Keys for Effective Preaching and Teaching
Of The Gospel

By
Dr. Elijah H. Hankerson III

On behalf of
Bishop Charles E. Blake, Sr.
Presiding Bishop and Chief Apostle

W*
WELSTAR PUBLICATIONS
· BROOKLYN, NEW YORK ·

Written by Dr. Elijah H. Hankerson III
Published by Welstar Publications, LLC.
Horace Batson, Publisher
628 Lexington Avenue, Brooklyn, NY 11221.
Phone: (646) 409-0340
Fax: (313) 453-6554
E-mail: publisher@welstarpublications.com
or drbatson@optonline.net
ISBN: 978-0-938503-38-5

Managing Editor, Frieda Arth
Book Design/Typography,
Text set in Georgia and Trajan Pro

Cover Design, Lori Monroe

TABLE OF CONTENTS

❖

Table of Contents

DEDICATION

*This book is dedicated to the
One Whom I serve, because He first loved me:*

THE LORD JESUS CHRIST

*And to (right after my salvation) the greatest joy of my life;
my family: My loving wife, Rachel, and children,
Elijah IV, Raquel, and Matthew*

ACKNOWLEDGEMENTS

❂

Special thanks to all of the individuals who helped, by their influence, to produce this book. Your impact upon my life is tremendously appreciated.

To the five great Gospel preachers who have influenced my life: Presiding Bishop Charles E. Blake, Sr., the late Bishop T. L. Westbrook, the late Bishop E. Harris Moore, Bishop R. J. Ward and the late Dr. Elijah H. Hankerson I.

To all of the former Presidents of the Department of Evangelism who have paved the way: The Bishop Lucius C. Page, the late Dr. Edward L. Battles, Bishop Richard "Mr. Clean" White, Admin. Asst. Dennis L. Martin, Sr. and Bishop Willie J. Campbell.

To those with which I labor shoulder to shoulder to spread this Gospel: The Life Center International C.O.G.I.C. family, the International Department of Evangelism family, the Robert C. Williams District family and the St. Louis Metropolitan Clergy Coalition family.

To (right after my salvation) the greatest joy of my life; my family: My loving wife, Rachel, and children, Elijah IV, Raquel, and Matthew.

To the One Whom I serve, because He first loved me: The LORD JESUS CHRIST

Every time I turn around, the Lord is blessing me!!!

FOREWORD

It is my joy to commend the Department of Evangelism of the Church Of God In Christ, for producing this book, which will aid in the work of the Lord.

Proverbs 29:18 says, *"Where there is no vision, the people perish."* In the Church Of God In Christ, God has provided a clear vision and purpose for our existence. We exist (1) to glorify God, (2) to win souls and (3) to edify believers.

The departments of our great church do not exist merely to have conventions and collect assessments. Training, resources and structure are provided to enable workers to fulfill our God-given vision.

Through the Department of Evangelism, the vital task of evangelizing the world is emphasized and fulfilled. This book provides principles of truth and training to aid those who preach and teach God's Word, so that they may be effective in winning souls.

As you read this book, expand your vision. We serve a great God. Expect to do great things for Him. Move beyond the vision of believing God for blocks and neighborhoods; start believing that your preaching and teaching ministry will impact nations!

I close these brief statements with some verses that have become somewhat of a theme of my life. May these words bless you in Isaiah 54:2-3, *"Enlarge the place of your tent, and let them stretch out the curtains of your dwellings; Do not spare; Lengthen your cords, and strengthen your stakes. For you shall expand to the right and to the left, and your descendants will inherit the nations, and make the desolate cities inhabited."*[1]

I see you in the future,

Bishop Charles E. Blake, Sr.
Seventh in Succession
Presiding Bishop
Church Of God In Christ, Inc.

---

1   Holy Bible. New King James Version. Thomas: Grand Rapids, 1982.

INTRODUCTION

The Department of Evangelism is the outreach wing of our great church: the Church Of God In Christ. It is through the evangelism and the preaching of the Word of God that souls are saved.

Only God can call and anoint a person to preach and teach His Word. However, it is our responsibility to sharpen our skills to that we can be effective at the delivery of the Gospel. The Lord has placed it upon the heart of our leader, Presiding Bishop Charles E. Blake, Sr., through the Department of Evangelism to present the material, contained in this booklet, to sharpen the skills of our preachers and teachers.

The purpose of this booklet, *Keys for Effective Preaching and Teaching of the Gospel* is to serve as a training tool for the ministry of the Word of God. The information is basic enough to sharpen the skills of beginning preachers and teachers. Yet, the information is thorough enough to serve as a "refresher" to those who have been laboring out in "the field" for many years.

On behalf of our Presiding Bishop (the most effective preacher of our time) and Department of Evangelism; may you be blessed as you learn the *Keys for Effective Preaching and Teaching of The Gospel.*

On behalf of Presiding Bishop Charles E. Blake Sr,
Leadership Team

Keys for Effective Preaching and Teaching
Of The Gospel

By
Dr. Elijah H. Hankerson III

On behalf of
Bishop Charles E. Blake, Sr.
Presiding Bishop and Chief Apostle

YOU MUST LIVE THE LIFE

❋

LESSON 1:

THE IMPORTANCE OF PRAYER

"Let us draw near with a true heart in full assurance of faith, having our hearts sprinkled from an evil conscience, and our bodies washed with pure water."

- HEBREWS 10:22 -

❋

LESSON 2:

YOU MUST BE FILLED WITH THE HOLY GHOST

❋

LESSON 3:

THE IMPORTANCE OF THE ANOINTING

"...And now, Lord, behold their threatenings: and grant unto thy servants, that with all boldness they may speak thy word..."

- ACTS 4:28-34 -

LESSON 1:

THE IMPORTANCE
OF PRAYER

(Unless otherwise indicated all Scripture quotations are from the King James Version of the Holy Bible)

❁

CONTENTS:

YOU HAVE ACCESS TO GOD

PRAYER IS THE KEY TO AN EFFECTIVE MINISTRY

PRAY IN FAITH

I.
YOU HAVE
ACCESS TO GOD!

❂

Hebrews 10:22 (King James Version). *Let us draw near with a true heart in full assurance of faith, having our hearts sprinkled from an evil conscience, and our bodies washed with pure water.*

GET AS CLOSE TO GOD AS YOU CAN!

If you are going to preach and teach God's Word, it is of necessity that you have an open line of communication with the Creator. Your ministry CANNOT be effective without a prayer life. Furthermore, *you do not want to just pray when it is time to preach or teach; you want to develop a consistent life of prayer.*

In our lesson Scripture, the "Hebrews" were former Jews that were about ready to abandon their new Christian faith. You may ask, "Why would they think of doing such a terrible thing?" The answer is that the criticism and persecution they endured, for becoming Christians, had become unbearable.

The writer of Hebrews (who is unknown) encouraged the "Hebrews" to get closer to God, instead of drawing back. He told them that the Christian faith was much better than their previous Jewish faith.

The difference between the "Hebrews" old Jewish faith and their new Christian faith had to do with accessibility to God (which was very difficult under the Old Covenant). Since the "Hebrews" could be close to God (because of what Jesus did) their relationship with God was supposed to be stronger, not weaker.[2]

How is it that the "Hebrews" (and actually any Christian) could get close to God? Our text is a part of a section (Hebrews 10:19-23) that teaches that under the New Covenant we are all "priests" and have a right to come into God's presence to minister and commune with Him. This is a privilege made possible by our being "sprinkled" by the blood of Jesus and "washed" by His Word![3]

Think about it, as "priests" God made us to fellowship with Him so that He can enjoy us! There are no earthly parents who enjoy the fellowship of their children more than God enjoys the fellowship of His children.[4] You have open access to God. You are His child and you can talk to Him (in prayer) any time! Praying with this type of confidence will make your preaching and teaching ministry effective.

YOU HAVE OPEN ACCESS TO GOD BECAUSE OF THE BLOOD OF JESUS!

Now there are many people who feel unworthy about having this kind of free access to God. And yes, it can be a very terrifying

---

2 Bell, James Stuart and Stan Campbell. The Complete Idiot's Guide to the Bible. Penguin: New York, 2005.

3 Dake, Finnis Jennings. Dake's Annotated Reference Bible. Lawrenceville: Dake, 2001.

4 Hagin, Kenneth E. Praying To Get Results. Rhema: Tulsa, 1983.

experience for fallen humanity to approach a holy and all-wise God. The Word does say, *Who only hath immortality, dwelling in the light which no man can approach unto; whom no man hath seen, nor can see: to whom be honour and power everlasting. Amen* (1 Timothy 6:6). Even Hebrews 10:31 says, *It is a fearful thing to fall into the hands of the living God.*

This is why God was about to kill Moses after his call to ministry, though called, Moses was still a fallen man in the presence of a holy God (Exodus 4:24). It was not until blood was shed (circumcision) that peace with God resumed (Exodus 4:25-26). In like manner only through the blood of Jesus Christ you have peace with God and have the freedom to approach Him without fear (Hebrews 9:22).

Jesus made it possible, through His blood, for you to not only approach God, but you can do it boldly and with the confidence that you have a right to be in His presence, and the privilege to fellowship with Him to receive help in your preaching and teaching ministry. Let us therefore come boldly unto the throne of grace, that we may obtain mercy, and find grace to help in time of need (Hebrews 4:16).

YOU HAVE OPEN ACCESS TO GOD BECAUSE JESUS IS YOUR MEDIATOR!

It is totally impossible for us to have any type of relationship with a holy God without an Intercessor. Remember a man in the Bible by the name of Job? He endured a great deal of challenges and wished that he had had an intercessor or a mediator to plead his case to God (Job 23:3-5). Thank God that you have a Mediator. In fact Jesus Christ is your...

A. Advocate (1 John 2:1). A person that pleads another's case.[5]

B. Intercessor (Hebrews 7:25). A person that argues on another's behalf.[6] (Compare this with Romans 8:26, 34).

C. Mediator (I Timothy 2:5). A person that helps opposing sides in an argument come to an agreement.[7]

YOU HAVE OPEN ACCESS TO GOD BECAUSE OF JESUS' NAME!

The Father will do anything for the Son (John 11:42). When I come to the Father in the Son's name (Jesus), it means that my relationship and fellowship with God is based on the Son's standing, merits, character and redemptive work. All of this is wonderful news that will refresh our confidence in approaching God and seeing our prayer lives and our faith soar to new heights. This news gives us the confidence to boldly go forth in the preaching and teaching of God's holy Word!

---

5   Mish, Frederick C. Webster's Ninth New Collegiate Dictionary. Webster: Springfield, 1989.

6   Ibid.

7   Ibid.

II.
PRAYER IS THE KEY TO AN
EFFECTIVE MINISTRY

❀

WHAT IS THE PURPOSE OF PRAYER?

We have already established the fact that we have a right to approach God in prayer because of what Jesus did for us. But, as preachers and teachers, why should we pray? Should we just pray to see all of our "prayer requests" granted?

While God is definitely concerned about your prayer requests, the purpose of prayer is not only to see our needs met. The ultimate aim is that through prayer we draw closer to God and become more like Him. That's important because it is better to "live" a sermon or a lesson, instead of just preaching or teaching one. Knowing that God wants you to be more like Him will encourage you, during times when it seems that your prayers are not being answered:

> *To pray is to change. Prayer is the central avenue God uses to transform us. If we are unwilling to change, we will abandon prayer as a noticeable characteristic of our lives. The closer we come to the heartbeat of God the more we see our need and the more we desire to be conformed to Christ[8].*

---

8   Foster, Richard. Celebration of Discipline. Harper: Cambridge: 1978.

HOW CAN YOUR PRAYERS BE MORE
EFFECTIVE AS A PREACHER OR TEACHER?

Again, although the purpose of prayer is for you to be closer to and more like God, He yet desires for your prayers to have results and for your ministry to be effective. This is why the Word teaches, *Confess to one another therefore your faults (your slips, your false steps, your offenses, your sins) and pray [also] for one another, that you may be healed and restored [to a spiritual tone of mind and heart]. The earnest (heartfelt, continued) prayer of a righteous man makes tremendous power available [dynamic in its working]* (James 5:16 Amplified Bible).⁹ Although we cannot, in this short lesson, give you every key to having an effective prayer life, here are six:

1. **To have an effective prayer life, speak the Word.** God honors His Word. Look at the prayers in the Bible that Jesus and the apostles prayed, put your name and the name of people on your prayer list in these prayers, then offer them up as a prayer to God. There is power in speaking the Word (read 1 Samuel 1:17, Matthew 8:8, 13, Mark 7:29). The following is an example of how you can pray the Word:

2. Ephesians 3:14-19. ¹⁴For this cause I bow my knees unto the Father of our Lord Jesus Christ, ¹⁵Of whom the whole family in heaven and earth is named, ¹⁶That he would grant (YOUR

---

9   Holy Bible. Amplified Version. Zondervan: Grand Rapids, 1987.

NAME), according to the riches of his glory, to be strengthened with might by his Spirit in the inner man; [17]That Christ may dwell in (YOUR NAME) hearts by faith; that (YOUR NAME), being rooted and grounded in love, [18]May be able to comprehend with all saints what is the breadth, and length, and depth, and height; [19]And to know the love of Christ, which passeth knowledge, that (YOUR NAME) might be filled with all the fulness of God.

3. **To have an effective prayer life, when you pray, call those things that be not, as though they are.** In no way is this lying or denying the *facts*; on the contrary, it is acknowledging and confessing the *truth* of God's Word. Romans 4:17 says, *(As it is written, I have made thee a father of many nations,) before him whom he believed, even God, who quickeneth the dead, and calleth those things which be not as though they were.*

4. **To have an effective prayer life - practice fasting.** In modern times fasting may seem extreme, but desperate needs will sometime require desperate measures. **Jesus said in Matthew 17:21,** *Howbeit this kind goeth not out but by prayer and fasting.* Always remember that the purpose of fasting is (1) reveal things that are controlling us, (2) reminds us that we are sustained by every Word of God, and (3) helps us to keep balance in our lives.[10]

---

10 Foster, Richard. Celebration of Discipline. Harper: Cambridge: 1978.

5. **To have an effective prayer life, keep your heart pure.** "Sin will keep prayer away, or else prayer will keep sin away."[11] _Isaiah 59:2 puts it this way, *But your iniquities have separated between you and your God, and your sins have hid his face from you, that he will not hear.* But, the good news in Hebrews 10:22 is that we have been "sprinkled" and "washed" from sin! People who have received inward cleansing from God can enjoy closeness or access to God.[12]

6. **To have an effective prayer life, you may face times of brokenness.** This writer has found that the times when his prayers have been the most effective, have been during times of distress and brokenness. Maybe this is why Hagee said, "God never forces you to do His will, but He often places you in extreme adversity that drives you to your knees and prepares you to do His will."[13] It was in a time of anguish that Jesus, the Son of God, prayed the prayer of consecration, *He went away again the second time, and prayed, saying, O my Father, if this cup may not pass away from me, except I drink it, thy will be done* (Matthew 26:42).

---

11 Zuck, Roy B. The Speaker's Quote Book. Kregel: Grand Rapids, 1997.

12 Bruce, F. F. The Epistle to the Hebrews. Eerdmans: Grand Rapids, 1990.

13 Hagee, John. The Seven Secrets. Charisma: Lake Mary, 2004.

III.
PRAY IN FAITH!

❂

WHAT IS FAITH?

You should have faith in God, that He will anoint and cause your preaching and teaching ministry to be effective! The biblical definition of faith is found in Hebrews 11:1, *Now faith is the substance of things hoped for, the evidence of things not seen.* What does this mean? It means that faith is (1) the solid reality of hope, (2) conviction about what you cannot see, (3) such awareness of God that you can endure all types of trouble.[14]

Yes, you can endure and overcome trouble, because faith (*Pistis*) is, "The truthfulness of God and reliance upon Christ for salvation." [15] [16] Faith is, "a life-long attitude of confident, un-questioning reliance and belief in every statement which comes from God."[17] [18] [19] In other words, true faith, "knows no hesitation in trusting and following Christ."[20]

---

14 Buttrick, Arthur George. The Interpreter's Dictionary of The Bible. New York: Abingdon, 1962.

15 Zodhiates, Spiros. The Complete Word Study New Testament. AMG: Chattanooga, 1991.

16 Vine, W. E. Vine's Complete Expository Dictionary of Old and New Testament Words. Nelson: Nashville, 1996.

17 Alexander, David. Eerdman's Handbook to the Bible. Eerdman's: Grand Rapids, 1973.

18 Mish, Frederick C. Webster's Ninth New Collegiate Dictionary. Webster: Springfield, 1989.

19 D. J. D. Davis Dictionary of The Bible. Royal: Nashville, 1973.

20 Hoerber, Robert G. Concordia Self-Study Bible. Concordia: St. Louis, 1986.

You may say, "I don't have unwavering faith like that." But, faith requires discipline and persistence.[21] To put it another way, you have to mix patience with your faith. Hebrews 6:12 says that it's through faith and patience that you inherit the promises of God. Also, James 1:3 teaches that the trying of your faith will produce patience.[22]

WITH FAITH, YOUR PRAYER LIFE AND MINISTRY WILL NEVER FAIL!

Your faith is the fuel that causes your prayers to ignite. Nothing will bring you near to God but believing, and nothing can shut you out from God but your unbelief...[23]

Your prayer life or your ministry can never be effective without this faith. James 1:6 says, *But let him ask in faith, nothing wavering. For he that wavereth is like a wave of the sea driven with the wind and tossed.*

According to Hebrews 10:22 our prayers will reach the Throne of God because we have "full assurance of faith." Here assurance (*plerophoria*) means, "to be certain, assured or incapable of failing!"[24] [25] [26] Do you see how exciting this is! When you exercise your faith, your prayers cannot fail!

21   Bell, James Stuart & Stan Campbell. The Complete Idiot's Guide to the Bible. Penguin: NY, 2005.

22   Hagin, Jr., Kenneth. I Cannot Be Defeated and I Will Not Quit. Rhema: Tulsa, 2001.

23   Carter, Tom. From the Writings of Charles H. Spurgeon. Baker: Grand Rapids, 1988.

24   Dake, Finnis Jennings. Dake's Annotated Reference Bible. Lawrenceville: Dake, 2001.

25   Mish, Frederick C. Webster's Ninth New Collegiate Dictionary. Webster: Springfield, 1989.

26   Strong, James. The Strongest Strong's. Zondervan: Grand Rapids, 2001.

THERE ARE THREE LEVELS OF FAITH

All of us should desire to exercise our faith, so that our prayers cannot fail. We should desire to have the highest level of faith ("great faith"):

A. No faith (Mark 4:40). *And he said unto them, Why are ye so fearful? How is it that ye have no faith?*

B. Little faith (Matthew 8:26). *And he saith unto them, Why are ye fearful, O ye of little faith? Then he arose, and rebuked the winds and the sea; and there was a great calm.*

C. Great faith (Matthew 8:10). *When Jesus heard it, he marvelled, and said to them that followed, Verily I say unto you, I have not found so great faith, no, not in Israel.*

HOW DO I GO FROM "NO FAITH" TO "GREAT FAITH?"

The good news is that you already have faith! Romans 12:3 says, *For I say, through the grace given unto me, to every man that is among you, not to think of himself more highly than he ought to think; but to think soberly, according as God hath dealt to every man the measure of faith.* You also have faith by receiving the Word of God. Romans 10:17 says, *So then faith cometh by hearing, and hearing by the word of God.*

But, to increase your level of faith (so that your prayer life and ministry can be effective) requires two things, (1) action and (2) love.

A. Faith is an action word.

Faith, in the book of Hebrews, is not just mental acceptance or verbal affirmation; faith actually means to press forward, based on trust in the promises of God (read all of Hebrews 11). Faith is a practical demonstration of your confidence in God and His Word. You cannot have faith without action; when you believe the Word, you have to also act on it.[27]Acting on faith is pressing forward as if everything depended upon you, but praying as if everything depended upon God. To put it another way, "Do your best and God will do the rest."[28]

B. Your faithwalk is related to your lovewalk.

In order for your faith to grow and be strong, it must be united with expressed love toward other people.[29] You may not think that love has anything to do with your faith or your prayer life; but your prayer life will be ineffective without expressed love toward those whom God has placed in your life:

---

27 Dollar, Creflo A. 8 Steps To Create The Life You Want. Faith Words: New York, 2008.

28 Carson, Ben, Think Big. Zondervan: Grand Rapids, 1992.

29 Thompson, Frank Charles. Thompson Chain Reference Bible. Thompson: Post Falls, n.d.

Galatians 5:6 *For in Jesus Christ neither circumcision availeth any thing, nor uncircumcision; but <u>faith which worketh by love.</u>*

1 John 3:23 *And this is his commandment, That we should <u>believe</u> on the name of his Son Jesus Christ, and <u>love</u> one another, as he gave us as commandment.*

1 Corinthians 13:4-7 gives three practical ways that you can express love:

1. **You can express love by being kind and patient with other people (1 Corinthians 14:4).** *Love endures long and is patient and kind; love never is envious nor boils over with jealousy, is not boastful or vainglorious, does not display itself haughtily.*

2. **You can express love by not being prideful or arrogant (1 Corinthians 13:5).** *It is not conceited (arrogant and inflated with pride); it is not rude (unmannerly) and does not act unbecomingly. Love (God's love in us) does not insist on its own rights or its own way, for it is not self-seeking; it is not touchy or fretful or resentful; it takes no account of the evil done to it [it pays no attention to a suffered wrong].*

C. **You can express love by being forgiving and merci-**

ful (1 Corinthians 13:6-7). *⁶It does not rejoice at injustice and unrighteousness, but rejoices when right and truth prevail. ⁷Love bears up under anything and everything that comes, is ever ready to believe the best of every person, its hopes are fadeless under all circumstances, and it endures everything [without weakening].*

Faith will keep you encouraged in your ministry when it seems like the door will stay locked.

In order to survive in the natural world you must rely on your five senses: touch, taste, smell, sight, sound. However, to overcome in the spiritual realm you must rely on your faith. For example, one writer has stated that, "faith is the bird that feels the light and sings to greet the dawn even while it is yet dark."[30]

---

30 Hewett, James S. Illustrations Unlimited. Tyndale: Wheaton, 1988.

LESSON 2:

YOU MUST BE FILLED WITH THE HOLY GHOST

(Unless otherwise indicated all Scripture quotations are from the Amplified version of the Holy Bible).[31]

❊

CONTENTS:

LESSON PURPOSE

DEFINITION OF THE BAPTISM OF THE HOLY GHOST

THE MOVEMENT OF THE HOLY GHOST IN THE LAST CENTURY

WHO IS THE HOLY SPIRIT?

THE BAPTISM OF THE HOLY SPIRIT

THE EFFECTS OF THE BAPTISM OF THE HOLY SPIRIT

---

31 KJV*Amplified Holy Bible Parallel Bible. Zondervan: Grand Rapids, 1995.

I.
LESSON PURPOSE

❀

This lesson will give you a basic understanding of the Baptism of the Holy Ghost, an experience essential for preachers and Bible teachers. This lesson is arranged somewhat differently from the others in this handbook, in that it mostly allows the Scriptures to speak for themselves.

II.
DEFINITIONS OF THE HOLY SPIRIT

❀

Old Testament. *Ruah.* Breath, air; strength; wind; breeze; spirit; courage; temper; Spirit. This noun cognates in Ugaritic, Aramaic, and Arabic. The word occurs about 378 times and in all periods of biblical Hebrew.[32]

New Testament. *Pnuema.* Primarily denotes "the wind" (akin to *pneo,* "to breath, blow"); also "breath"; then, especially "the spirit," which, like the wind, is invisible, immaterial and powerful. The "Holy Spirit" is spoken of under various titles in the NT ("Spirit" and "Ghost"

---

32 Vine, W. E. Vine's Complete Expository Dictionary of Old and New Testament Words. Nelson: Nashville, 1996.

are renderings of the same word, *pnuema*: the advantage of the rendering "Spirit" is that it can always be used, whereas "Ghost" always requires the word "Holy" prefixed.) In the following list the omission of the definite article marks its omission in the original:

- Spirit (Matthew 22:43)

- Eternal Spirit (Hebrews 9:14)

- The Spirit (Matthew 4:1).

- Holy Spirit (Matthew 1:18)

- the Holy Spirit (Matthew 28:19)

- the Spirit of promise (Ephesians 1:13).

- Spirit of God (Romans 8:9)

- Spirit of the living God (2 Corinthians 3:3)

- the Spirit of God (1 Corinthians 2:11)

- the Spirit of our God (1 Corinthians 6:11)

- the Spirit of glory and of God (1 Peter 4:14)

- the Spirit of Him that raised up Jesus from the dead

- (Romans 8:11)

- the Spirit of your Father (Matthew 10:20)

- the Spirit of His Son (Galatians 4:6)

- Spirit of the Lord (Acts 8:39)

- the Spirit of the Lord (Acts 5:9)

- the Lord, the Spirit (2 Corinthians 3:18)

- the Spirit of Jesus (Acts 16:7)

- Spirit of Christ (Romans 8:9)

- the Spirit of Jesus Christ (Philemon 1:19)

- Spirit of adoption (Romans 8:15)

- the Spirit of truth (John 14:17)

- the Spirit of life (Romans 8:2)

- the Spirit of grace (Hebrews 10:29)[33]

BIBLE DICTIONARY[34]

The Spirit of God is the divine principle of activity everywhere at work in the world, executing the will of God.

The Spirit is sent forth by God and given by God (Numbers 11:29). The Spirit brooded over chaotic matter in the beginning and is everywhere present (Genesis 1:2), and is thus immanent and the energy in cosmical processes (Job 26:13); is able to produce supernatural effects (1 Kings 34:14; 2 Kings 2:6).

He abides with the people of God (Haggai 2:5), and bestows varied powers for the work of the kingdom, strength (Judges 3:10),

---

33 Vine, W. E. Vine's Complete Expository Dictionary of Old and New Testament Words. Nelson: Nashville, 1996.

34 D., J. D. Illustrated Davis Dictionary of the Bible. Royal: Nashville, 1973.

wisdom (Numbers 11:17, 25), in short, everything needful for the work of the kingdom (Isaiah 11:2).

He instructed the people of God (Nehemiah 9:20) by inspiring the prophets (Numbers 24:2). He works upon the heart of the individual child of God.

It was foretold that this work would be especially powerful and widespread in the Messianic period, when the Spirit shall be poured out on the people of God, will give them a new heart and a new spirit (Ezekiel 34:26), produce sorrow for sin (Zechariah 11:10) and be poured out on all flesh (Joel 2:28).

The New Testament talks of Messianic times and the dispensation of the Spirit, and consequently the Spirit is mentioned more often in the New Testament than in the Old Testament. All the attributes of the Spirit revealed in the Old Testament are disclosed in the New Testament in exercise. The doctrine of the Spirit advances beyond the teaching of the Old Testament chiefly in becoming more definite in respect to His personality.

BIBLE HANDBOOK.[35]

The Holy Spirit is one with God the Father and Jesus Christ, actively at working the world of men, particularly in and through God's people.

---

35   Alexander, David. Eerdman's Handbook of the Bible. Eerdman's: Grand Rapids, 1973.

III.
DEFINITION OF THE
BAPTISIM OF THE HOLY SPIRIT

❋

The Baptism of the Holy Spirit is an experience subsequent to conversion and sanctification and tongue speaking is the consequence of the Baptism of the Holy Spirit.[36] It is important to note that all "Full Gospel" movements in America believe in some version of this important biblical doctrine, including, but not limited to:

- Bible Way Churches Worldwide
- Church Of God (Cleveland, TN)
- Church Of God In Christ
- Church Of God Of Prophecy
- Church Of Our Lord Jesus Christ Of The Apostolic Faith
- Higher Ground Always Abounding Assemblies
- International Church Of The Foursquare Gospel
- General Council Of The Assemblies of God
- Open Bible Standard Church
- Pentecostal Assemblies Of Canada

---

36 Range, C. F. Official Manual of the Doctrines and Discipline of the Church Of God In Christ. COGIC Publishing House: Memphis, 1973.

- Pentecostal Assemblies Of The World
- Pentecostal Church Of God
- Pentecostal Holiness Church International
- United Pentecostal Church International

THE MOVEMENT OF THE HOLY SPIRIT
IN THE LAST CENTURY

A.　**Topeka, Kansas and Charles Fox Parham.**[37] Charles F. Parham encouraged students at this Bethel Bible School in Topeka, Kansas, to pray for the gift of tongues. He had been inspired by the spiritual dynamics of the New Testament church, as recorded in the Book of Acts. Along with his students (Agnes Ozman was the first); he was baptized in the Spirit and spoke in tongues in early January, 1901.

An independent preacher in the Holiness movement, he forged his most enduring legacy by noting that tongues marks the "Bible evidence" of Spirit baptism in the book of Acts, later referred to by Pentecostals as the "initial evidence."

B.　**Los Angeles, California and William Joseph Seymour.**[38] Seymour was invited to pastor in Los Angeles.

37　McGhee, Gary. "The Holy Spirit Falls at Topeka." Pentecostal Evangel. General Council: Springfield, May 31, 1998.

38　Horn, Ken. "The Azusa Street Revival." Pentecostal Evangel. General Council: Springfield, May 31, 1998.

Though many accepted the teaching (about the Baptism of the Holy Spirit), he was locked out of the church. He moved to a private house on Bonnie Brae Street to preach. (This house is now owned by the California Southern First Jurisdiction of the Church Of God In Christ).

Here, on April 9, 1906, seven worshippers were struck by the power of God and began to speak in other tongues. Soon people of all races and from a rich variety of church backgrounds were attracted – and many spoke in tongues. It initially produced a movement that was colorblind. Soon word spread and the Bonnie Brae house was too small.

The meetings moved to an old building that originally had been an AME church at 312 Azusa Street. This became the home of the revival. People visited the Apostolic Faith Gospel Mission (Aka "Azusa Street") there in large numbers. There was continuous revival for three years. It was not uncommon for a meeting to go from 10:00 a.m. until midnight.

WHO IS THE HOLY SPIRIT?

2 Corinthians 3:17. Now the Lord is the Spirit, and where the Spirit of the Lord is, there is liberty (emancipation from bondage, freedom). [Isa. 61:1, 2.]

The Baptism of the Holy Spirit

A. The Baptism of the Holy Spirit is known by two different terms.

Matthew 3:11. I indeed baptize you in (with) water because of repentance [that is, because of your changing your minds for the better, heartily amending your ways, with abhorrence of your past sins]. But He Who is coming after me is mightier than I, Whose sandals I am not worthy or fit to take off or carry; He will baptize you with the Holy Spirit and with fire.

Acts 2:4. And they were all filled (diffused throughout their souls) with the Holy Spirit and began to speak in other (different, foreign) languages (tongues), as the Spirit kept giving them clear and loud expression [in each tongue in appropriate words].

B. The necessity of the Baptism of the Holy Spirit.

Luke 24:49. And behold, I will send forth upon you what My Father has promised; but remain in the city [Jerusalem] until you are clothed with power from on high.

Acts 8:14-17. 14Now when the apostles (special messengers) at Jerusalem heard that [the country of] Samaria had accepted and welcomed the Word of God, they sent Peter and John to them, 15And they came down and prayed for them that the Samaritans might receive the Holy Spirit; [16]For He had not yet fallen upon any of them, but they had only been baptized into the name of the Lord Jesus. [17]Then [the apostles] laid their hands on them one by one, and they received the Holy Spirit.

Romans 8:9. But you are not living the life of the flesh, you are living the life of the Spirit, if the [Holy] Spirit of God [really] dwells within you [directs and controls you]. But if anyone does not possess the [Holy] Spirit of Christ, he is none of His [he does not belong to Christ, is not truly a child of God].

Romans 8:16. The Spirit Himself [thus] testifies together with our own spirit, [assuring us] that we are children of God.

1 John 4:13. By this we come to know (perceive, recognize, and understand) that we abide (live and remain) in Him and He in us: because He has given (imparted) to us of His [Holy] Spirit.

C.   **The purpose of the Baptism of the Holy Spirit.**

Acts 1:8. But you shall receive power (ability, efficiency, and might) when the Holy Spirit has come upon you, and you shall be My witnesses in Jerusalem and all Judea and Samaria and to the ends (the very bounds) of the earth.

D. **The evidence of the Baptism of the Holy Spirit.**

Acts 2:4. And they were all filled (diffused throughout their souls) with the Holy Spirit and began to speak in other (different, foreign) languages (tongues), as the Spirit kept giving them clear and loud expression [in each tongue in appropriate words].

E. **How do you receive the Baptism of the Holy Spirit?**

Galatians 3:2. Let me ask you this one question: Did you receive the [Holy] Spirit as the result of obeying the Law and doing its works, or was it by hearing [the message of the Gospel] and believing [it]? [Was it from observing a law of rituals or from a message of faith?]

F. **Example of people who received the Baptism of the Holy Spirit in the Bible.**

Acts 2:4. And they were all filled (diffused throughout their souls) with the Holy Spirit and began to speak in other (different, foreign) languages (tongues), as the Spirit kept giving them clear and loud expression [in each tongue in appropriate words].

Acts 10:44-46. 44 While Peter was still speaking these words, the Holy Spirit fell on all who were listening to the message. 45And the believers from among the circumcised [the Jews] who came with Peter were surprised and amazed, because the free gift of the Holy Spirit had been bestowed and poured out largely even on the Gentiles. 46For they heard them talking in [unknown] tongues (languages) and extolling and magnifying God. Then Peter asked...

G. How did people receive the Baptism of the Holy Spirit in the Bible?

Acts 1:14. All of these with their minds in full agreement devoted themselves steadfastly to prayer, [waiting together] with the women and Mary the mother of Jesus, and with His brothers.

Acts 8:17. Then [the apostles] laid their hands on them one by one, and they received the Holy Spirit.

Acts 9:17-18. 17So Ananias left and went into the house. And he laid his hands on Saul and said, Brother Saul, the Lord Jesus, Who appeared to you along the way by which you came here, has sent me that you may recover your sight and be filled with the Holy Spirit. 18And instantly something like scales fell from [Saul's] eyes, and he recovered his sight. Then he arose and was baptized...

Acts 10:44. While Peter was still speaking these words, the Holy Spirit fell on all who were listening to the message.

Acts 19:6. And as Paul laid his hands upon them, the Holy Spirit came on them; and they spoke in [foreign, unknown] tongues (languages) and prophesied.

H. Is water baptism associated with the Baptism of the Holy Spirit?

Acts 19:5-6. 5On hearing this they were baptized [again, this time] in the name of the Lord Jesus. 6And as Paul laid his hands upon them, the Holy Spirit came on them; and they spoke in [foreign, unknown] tongues (languages) and prophesied.

I. The Baptism of the Holy Spirit is for believers of all times.

Acts 2:39. For the promise [of the Holy Spirit] is to and for you and your children, and to and for all that are far away, [even] to and for as many as the Lord our God invites and bids to come to Himself.

J. What are the prerequisites for receiving the Baptism of the Holy Spirit?

Acts 2:38. And Peter answered them, Repent (change your views and purpose to accept the will of God in your inner selves instead of rejecting it) and be baptized, every one of you, in the name of Jesus Christ for the forgiveness of and release from your sins; and you shall receive the gift of the Holy Spirit.

K. When should a person receive the Baptism of the Holy Spirit?

Acts 19:2. And he asked them, Did you receive the Holy Spirit when you believed [on Jesus as the Christ]? And they said, No, we have not even heard that there is a Holy Spirit.

L. How do you speak in tongues?

Acts 2:4. And they were all filled (diffused throughout their souls) with the Holy Spirit and began to speak in other (different, foreign) languages (tongues), as the Spirit kept giving them clear and loud expression [in each tongue in appropriate words].

M. Why should you speak in tongues?
James 3:8. But the human tongue can be tamed by no man. It is a restless (undisciplined, irreconcilable) evil, full of deadly poison.

N. Will the Holy Spirit have you to express yourself in an emotional manner?

Acts 2:13. But others made a joke of it and derisively said, They are simply drunk and full of sweet [intoxicating] wine.

Acts 2:46. And day after day they regularly assembled in the temple with united purpose, and in their homes they broke bread [including the Lord's Supper]. They partook of their food with gladness and simplicity and generous hearts...

THE EFFECTS OF THE BAPTISM OF THE HOLY SPIRIT

A.   **The benefits of having the Baptism of the Holy Spirit.**

John 7:37-39. 37Now on the final and most important day of the Feast, Jesus stood, and He cried in a loud voice, If any man is thirsty, let him come to Me and drink! 38He who believes in Me [who cleaves to and trusts in and relies on Me] as the Scripture has said, From his innermost being shall flow [continuously] springs and rivers of living water. 39But He was speaking here of the Spirit, Whom those who believed (trusted, had faith) in Him were afterward to receive. For the [Holy] Spirit had not yet been given, because Jesus was not yet glorified (raised to honor).

John 14:16. And I will ask the Father, and He will give you another Comforter (Counselor, Helper, Intercessor, Advocate, Strengthener, and Standby), that He may remain with you forever--

John 14:26. But the Comforter (Counselor, Helper, Intercessor, Advocate, Strengthener, Standby), the Holy Spirit, Whom the Father will send in My name [in My place, to represent Me and act on My behalf], He will teach you all things. And He will cause you to recall (will remind you of, bring to your remembrance) everything I have told you.

B.   Characteristics of someone who is filled with the Holy Spirit.

Acts 1:8. But you shall receive power (ability, efficiency, and might) when the Holy Spirit has come upon you, and you shall be My witnesses in Jerusalem and all Judea and Samaria and to the ends (the very bounds) of the earth.

Romans 14:17. [After all] the kingdom of God is not a matter of [getting the] food and drink [one likes], but instead it is righteousness (that state which makes a person acceptable to God) and [heart] peace and joy in the Holy Spirit.

Galatians 5:22-24. 22But the fruit of the [Holy] Spirit [the work which His presence within accomplishes] is love, joy (gladness), peace, patience (an even temper, forbearance), kindness, goodness (benevolence), faithfulness, 23Gentleness (meekness, humility), self-control (self-restraint, continence). Against such things there is no law [that can bring a charge].24And those who belong to Christ Jesus (the Messiah) have crucified the flesh (the godless human nature) with its passions and appetites and desires.

C.   People who receive the Holy Spirit have supernatural gifts.

Romans 12:6-8. 6Having gifts (faculties, talents, qualities) that differ according to the grace given us, let us use them: [He whose gift is] prophecy, [let him prophesy] according to the proportion of his faith;   7[He whose gift is] practical service, let him give himself to serving; he who teaches, to his teaching; 8He who exhorts (encourages), to his exhortation; he who contributes, let him do it in simplicity and liberality; he who gives aid and superintends, with zeal and singleness of mind; he who does acts of mercy, with genuine cheerfulness and joyful eagerness.

1 Corinthians 12:7-10. 7But to each one is given the manifestation of the [Holy] Spirit [the evidence, the spiritual illumination of the Spirit] for good and profit. 8To one is given in and through the [Holy] Spirit [the power to speak] a message of wisdom, and to another [the power to express] a word of knowledge and understanding according to the same [Holy] Spirit; 9To another [wonder-working] faith by the same [Holy] Spirit, to another the extraordinary powers of healing by the one Spirit;10To another the working of miracles, to another prophetic insight (the gift of interpreting the divine will and purpose); to another the ability to discern and distinguish between [the utterances of true] spirits [and false ones], to another various kinds of [unknown] tongues, to another the ability to interpret [such] tongues.

LESSON 3:

THE IMPORTANCE OF
THE ANOINTING

(Unless otherwise indicated all Scripture quotations are from the Amplified version of the Holy Bible).[39]

❁

CONTENTS:

INTRODUCTION

UNDERSTANDING THE BOOK OF ACTS

FACTS ABOUT THE ANOINTING

---

39   KJV*Amplified Holy Bible Parallel Bible. Zondervan: Grand Rapids, 1995.

I.
INTRODUCTION

(Unless otherwise indicated all Scripture quotations are from the King James Version of the Holy Bible)

❋

Acts 4:28-34. [28]For to do whatsoever thy hand and thy counsel determined before to be done. [29]And now, Lord, behold their threatenings: and grant unto thy servants, that with all boldness they may speak thy word, [30]By stretching forth thine hand to heal; and that signs and wonders may be done by the name of thy holy child Jesus. [31]And when they had prayed, the place was shaken where they were assembled together; and they were all filled with the Holy Ghost, and they spake the word of God with boldness. [32]And the multitude of them that believed were of one heart and of one soul: neither said any of them that ought of the things which he possessed was his own; but they had all things common. [33]And with great power gave the apostles witness of the resurrection of the Lord Jesus: and great grace was upon them all. [34]Neither was there any among them that lacked: for as many as were possessors of lands or houses sold them, and brought the prices of the things that were sold,

PURPOSE OF THIS LESSON

No preacher, teacher, ministry or anyone serving in leadership in the Church can be effective without the presence of God.

This message is designed to help you to realize that in order to obtain and maintain the Presence of God, you must be desperate for Him.

The topic we are discussing is very important because we have learned to "do church" without the Presence. We have mistaken manifestations for the Presence. For when the true Presence shows up there will be a change. Falling out means nothing, unless people get up a different way! Shaking means nothing, if you remain bound! Tongue speaking is meaningless, if we can't speak English to each other!

At this point you may ask, "What is the Presence." The anointing is the Presence. The anointing is the Presence of God upon a person's life or ministry; causing yokes of bondage to be destroyed. Consider the following passages:

Isaiah 10:27. *And it shall come to pass in that day, that his burden shall be taken away from off thy shoulder, and his yoke from off thy neck, and the yoke shall be destroyed because of the anointing.*

Acts 10:38. *How God anointed Jesus of Nazareth with the Holy Ghost and with power: who went about doing good, and healing all that were oppressed of the devil; for God was with him.*

Now let's move on and find out more about the book of Acts and a simple explanation of our text.

II.
UNDERSTANDING
THE BOOK OF ACTS

❀

THE AUTHOR OF ACTS WAS LUKE THE PHYSICIAN

Luke the physician wrote both the Gospel According to Luke and the book of Acts; as is explained in Luke 1:3-4 and Acts 1:1. They were actually a two volume series sometimes referred to as Luke-Acts.

Surprisingly, Luke is the only non-Jewish writer in the New Testament.[40]He was not one of the 12 apostles, but he travelled with the apostle Paul.[41] This is why there are several points in Acts at which the story shifts from "they" to "we."[42]

WHO WAS THEOPHILUS?

Both Luke and Acts were dedicated to a Roman by the name of Theophilus. Luke wanted to give Theophilus an accurate record of the true facts about Christianity (Luke 1:1-4); because there werea lot of strange and distorted rumors about the faith.[43]

---

40 Alexander, David. Eerdman's Handbook to the Bible. Eerdman's: Grand Rapids, 1973.

41 Bell, James Stuart and Stan Campbell. The Complete Idiot's Guide to the Bible. Penguin: New York, 2005.

42 White, L. Michael. From Jesus To Christianity. Harper: New York, 2004.

43 Ibid.

Luke-Acts was also intentionally produced for wider distribution. This is also why the book is dedicated to Theophilus, because he paid to have these books produced.

It was a normal practice to dedicate books like Luke-Acts to the "patron" or corporate sponsor who paid for the publication (that is, the cost of the papyrus, ink, secretaries, copyists and even the support of the author). It was therefore an enormous cost to produce and publish a work the size of the book of Luke-Acts.[44]

WHY WAS ACTS WRITTEN?

The book of Acts informs us of what occurred among believers between the four Gospels and the later letters. In the Gospel According to Luke, Luke says he dealt with all that Jesus began to do and teach (Acts 1:1). In Acts Luke describes what Jesus continued to do and teach through the Church.[45] Since the apostles lead this movement, the book is often referred to as the Acts of the Apostles. However, the "acts" or deeds are mainly those of the apostles Peter and Paul.[46] Acts covers a period of thirty years, from the birth of the church on the Day of Pentecost to the close of Paul's imprisonment at Rome. Acts 4:28-34 describes how the church received a refilling of the Holy Ghost (the anointing), during a time of intense persecution. Let's go on and learn more about the anointing.

44 White, L. Michael. From Jesus To Christianity. Harper: New York, 2004.

45 Unger, Merrill. The New Unger's Bible Handbook. Moody: Chicago, 1998.

46 Alexander, David. Eerdman's Handbook to the Bible. Eerdman's: Grand Rapids, 1973.

III.

FACTS ABOUT THE ANOINTING

❂

We have already learned that the anointing is the Presence of God upon a person's life or ministry; causing yokes of bondage to be destroyed. It is the anointing, which brings supernatural results. Here are some facts and reminders about the anointing:

A.   **The anointing cannot be duplicated or fabricated.** "You can fake the anointing – but you cannot fake the results."[47]

B.   **The anointing is transferable.** As in the story of Elijah and Elisha.

> **2 Kings 2:8-9. 8**And Elijah took his mantle, and wrapped it together, and smote the waters, and they were divided hither and thither, so that they two went over on dry ground. 9And it came to pass, when they were gone over, that Elijah said unto Elisha, Ask what I shall do for thee, before I be taken away from thee. And Elisha said, I pray thee, let a double portion of thy spirit be upon me.

---

47 Source unknown.

C.   **The anointing is increasable.** Especially through the discipline of fasting. In modern times fasting may seem extreme; but desperate needs will sometime require desperate measures. Jesus said in Matthew 17:21, Howbeit this kind goeth not out but by prayer and fasting.

Always remember that the purpose of fasting (1) reveals things that are controlling us, (2) reminds us that we are sustained by every Word of God, and (3) helps us to keep balance in our lives.[48]

D.   **The anointing is costly.** As Elijah tried to tell Elisha.

> **2 Kings 2:10.** And he said, Thou hast asked a hard thing: nevertheless, if thou see me when I am taken from thee, it shall be so unto thee; but if not, it shall not be so.

E.   **The anointing functions at various levels.** God does not always anoint you at the same level.

F.   **You are not under the anointing 24/7.** You have to know how to relate to the natural realm also.

---

48   Foster, Richard. Celebration of Discipline. Harper: Cambridge: 1978.

YOUR MOTIVES MUST BE PURE

✦

LESSON 4:

MAKE SURE YOU MAINTAIN THE RIGHT SPIRIT

✦

LESSON 5:

MINISTRY IS ABOUT SERVING

"Jesus knowing that the Father had given all things into his hands, and that he was come from God, and went to God; ⁴He riseth from supper, and laid aside his garments; and took a towel, and girded himself. ⁵After that he poureth water into a bason, and began to wash the disciples' feet, and to wipe them with the towel wherewith he was girded..."

- JOHN 13:3-5, 12-15 -

LESSON 4:

MAKE SURE YOU MAINTAIN THE RIGHT SPIRIT

(Unless otherwise indicated all Scripture quotations are from the King James Version of the Holy Bible)

❁

CONTENTS:

UNDERSTANDING PROTOCOL

RENEW A RIGHT SPIRIT WITHIN ME

I.

UNDERSTANDING PROTOCOL

(Unless otherwise indicated all Scripture quotations are from the King James Version of the Holy Bible)

❂

WORKING IN A JURISDICTION

Always remember, as a preacher and Bible teacher, that it is a blessing and privilege to be asked to do any type of service in the Kingdom of God. If we keep this in mind, we will always be assured of being successful, in all levels of Kingdom work.

This lesson will help to ensure that you are successful in your endeavor by teaching you how to have the right type of spirit that will ensure success.

THE RULES OF PROTOCOL IN THE CHURCH OF GOD IN CHRIST

Before we go on, however, let's address a subject that is very important in the Church Of God In Christ, if you are going to be successful in ministry in this denomination.

Our forefathers taught that familiarity breeds contempt. This truth prevails in every area of life. It is therefore in that same spirit that it is insisted that Church Of God In Christ workers never seek to be "familiar" with their superiors. Unsolicited interferences in the conversations of the superiors are a mark of ignorance and disrespect.

Because of their close proximity to the Jurisdictional Bishop and the Supervisor for the Department of Women, workers must learn to work in the company of the Church-fathers, and hear only that which is spoken to them. They must never repeat any matter they happen to overhear, without the leader's consent.

Your leader is to be referred to by his highest title and last name. Nicknames are never to be used in public or private. First name basis with your Jurisdictional Bishop or Supervisor for the Department of Women is out of order. The superior may refer to you by your first name, but you must always respond to him with "sir" or "Bishop."[49]

---

49   Thuston, Bishop Lemuel F. Church Of God In Christ National Adjutancy. N.P., 1998.

II.
RENEW A RIGHT SPIRIT WITHIN ME

❀

SPIRITS THAT PREACHERS AND BIBLE TEACHERS SHOULD NOT HAVE

A. **Do not have a "spirit of Korah."** This spirit causes an insurrection amongst leadership. It refuses to give honor and respect to whom it is due, because it makes a person feel that they are equal in status, station and call to their leader.[50]

Numbers 16:1-3 (Contemporary English Version). 1-2 Korah son of Izhar was a Levite from the Kohathite clan. One day he called together Dathan, Abiram, and On from the Reuben tribe, and the four of them decided to rebel against Moses. So they asked two hundred fifty respected Israelite leaders for their support, and together they went to Moses 3and Aaron and said, "Why do you think you're so much better than anyone else? We're part of the LORD's holy people, and he's with all of us. What makes you think you're the only ones in charge?"

---

50   Trimm, Dr. Cindy N. Binding the Strong Man. Kingdom Life: Ft Lauderdale, 2005.

B.   Do not have a "spirit of Absalom." This is a renegade spirit. This spirit is cunning and causes a person to undermine and usurp authority. It divides and conquers transferring loyalty from one person to another.[51]

2 Samuel 15:1-6 (Contemporary English Version). 1Some time later, Absalom got himself a chariot with horses to pull it, and he had fifty men run in front. 2He would get up early each morning and wait by the side of the road that led to the city gate. Anyone who had a complaint to bring to King David would have to go that way, and Absalom would ask each of them, "Where are you from?" If they said, "I'm from a tribe in the north," 3Absalom would say, "You deserve to win your case. It's too bad the king doesn't have anyone to hear complaints like yours. 4I wish someone would make me the judge around here! I would be fair to everyone." 5Whenever anyone would come to Absalom and start bowing down, he would reach out and hug and kiss them. 6That's how he treated everyone from Israel who brought a complaint to the king. Soon everyone in Israel liked Absalom better than they liked David.

C.   Do not have a "spirit of Ahithophel." This is a spirit that betrays a leader due to personal ambition.

2 Samuel 15:12 (The Message). While Absalom was offering sacrifices, he managed also to involve Ahithophel the Gilonite,

---

51   Ibid.

David's advisor, calling him away from his hometown of Giloh. The conspiracy grew powerful and Absalom's supporters multiplied.

D. **Do not have a "spirit of Judas."** This spirit seeks to betray and make a mockery of the leader for personal ambition. As one that has the privilege to be close to your leader, you should never try to betray your leader's weaknesses for personal gain, but should uphold him in prayer.

Matthew 26:14-16, 47-50 (New King James Version). 14 Then one of the twelve, called Judas Iscariot, went to the chief priests 15 and said, "What are you willing to give me if I deliver Him to you?" And they counted out to him thirty pieces of silver. 16 So from that time he sought opportunity to betray Him. 47 And while He was still speaking, behold, Judas, one of the twelve, with a great multitude with swords and clubs, came from the chief priests and elders of the people. 48 Now His betrayer had given them a sign, saying, "Whomever I kiss, He is the One; seize Him." 49 Immediately he went up to Jesus and said, "Greetings, Rabbi!" and kissed Him. 50 But Jesus said to him, "Friend, why have you come?" Then they came and laid hands on Jesus and took Him.

E. **Do not have a critical, faultfinding, grumbling and complaining spirit.** This is a spirit that instead of standing with the leader, seeks to find fault with everything he does.

Numbers 21:5-7 (New Living Translation). 5 and they began to speak against God and Moses. "Why have you brought us out of Egypt to die here in the wilderness?" they complained. "There is nothing to eat here and nothing to drink. And we hate this horrible manna!" 6 So the LORD sent poisonous snakes among the people, and many were bitten and died. 7 Then the people came to Moses and cried out, "We have sinned by speaking against the LORD and against you. Pray that the LORD will take away the snakes." So Moses prayed for the people.

THE TYPE OF SPIRIT PREACHERS AND BIBLE TEACHERS SHOULD HAVE.

A.   An obedient spirit.
Hebrews 13:17 (King James Version). Obey them that have the rule over you, and submit yourselves: for they watch for your souls, as they that must give account, that they may do it with joy, and not with grief: for that is unprofitable for you.

B.   A friendly spirit.
Proverbs 18:24 (King James Version). A man that hath friends must shew himself friendly: and there is a friend that sticketh closer than a brother.

C.   **An excellent spirit.**

Daniel 6:3 (King James Version). Then this Daniel was preferred above the presidents and princes, because an excellent spirit was in him; and the king thought to set him over the whole realm.

D.   **A dependable spirit.**

Ephesians 6:21-22 (The Message).[52] 21-22Tychicus, my good friend here, will tell you what I'm doing and how things are going with me. He is certainly a dependable servant of the Master! I've sent him not only to tell you about us but to cheer you on in your faith.

E.   **A humble spirit.**

Numbers 12:3 (King James Version). Now the man Moses was very meek, above all the men which were upon the face of the earth.

---

52   Peterson, Eugene E. The Message. NAV: Colorado Springs, 2005.

LESSON 5:

MINISTRY IS ABOUT SERVING

*(Unless otherwise indicated all Scripture quotations are from
the King James Version of the Holy Bible)*

❁

CONTENTS:

PREACHERS AND TEACHERS MUST BE SERVANTS

SERVING IN "ANOTHER MAN'S HOUSE"

THE CHARACTERISTICSOF A GODLY SERVANT

I.

PREACHERS AND TEACHERS
MUST BE SERVANTS

*(Unless otherwise indicated all Scripture quotations
are from the King James Version of the Holy Bible)*

❁

John 13:3-5, 12-15. *3Jesus knowing that the Father had
given all things into his hands, and that he was come from God, and
went to God; 4He riseth from supper, and laid aside his garments;
and took a towel, and girded himself. 5After that he poureth water
into a bason, and began to wash the disciples' feet, and to wipe
them with the towel wherewith he was girded. 12So after he had
washed their feet, and had taken his garments, and was set down
again, he said unto them, Know ye what I have done to you? 13Ye
call me Master and Lord: and ye say well; for so I am. 14If I then,
your Lord and Master, have washed your feet; ye also ought to
wash one another's feet. 15For I have given you an example, that ye
should do as I have done to you.*

TO BE A MANAGER, YOU HAVE
TO START AT THE BOTTOM – NO EXCEPTIONS.

~ HENRY BLOCK ~

Henry Block, CEO of H & R Block, started his company with
only his training in mathematics and bookkeeping. Initially, his

only competition was taxpayers who filled out their own returns. Currently, H & R Block is a multi-million dollar company and the leader in its industry.

Block was able to build this major corporation, because of his commitment to the principle of servanthood. [53] Similarly, because of Jesus' commitment to servanthood, our sins are forgiven and we have eternal life. This was symbolized in the ordinance of Footwashing.

WHAT DOES FOOTWASHING SYMBOLIZE?

The root of this practice appears to be found in the hospitality customs of ancient civilizations, especially where sandals were the chief footwear. A host would provide water for guests to wash their feet, serve the guests by washing their feet, or even provide a servant to wash the feet of the guests. [54]

To wash another person's feet was symbolic of being a servant. Jesus of course performed the ultimate sign of servanthood by humbling Himself and dying on the Cross (Mark 10:43-44).

DO I HAVE TO DO EVERYTHING MYSELF?

Even though John 13:2 says that the washing of feet occurred once supper had ended, a better translation would be

---

53 Van Crouch Communications. The C.E.O.'s Little Instruction Book. Trade Life: Tulsa, 1999.

54 http://en.wikipedia.org/wiki/Footwashing. (Accessed, September 9, 2009).

"the end of the preparation for supper."[55] It was always before the ceremonial meal that the participants would wash their feet; it was probably at this point that Jesus washed His disciples' feet.[56]

There was obviously no servant present and none of the disciples were going to volunteer. It was necessary for Jesus to wash feet because at this sacred time of Passover (and right before His own suffering and death); instead of His disciple's being consecrated, or showing any compassion for each other, they were too busy arguing over who would be the greatest.[57]

ARE YOU INTO TITLES OR TOWELS?

Jesus knew who He was and He was secure enough to get down on the floor and wash His disciples' feet. No one else had volunteered to do the job, so Jesus saw a need and met it.[58]

Jesus didn't have anything to prove. He had nothing to lose and nothing to hide. The insecure are into titles. The secure are into towels. Jesus' security enabled Him to both stoop and stretch.

---

55 Dake, Finis Jennings. Dake's Annotated Reference Bible. Dake: Lawrenceville, 2001.

56 Alexander, David, Ed. Eerdman's Handbook to the Bible. Eerdman's: Grand Rapids, 1973.

57 Hoerber, Robert G. Concordia Self-Study Bible New International Version. Concordia: Saint Louis, 1986.

58 Maxwell, John. The Maxwell Leadership Bible. Nelson: Nashville, 2007.

WHAT IS THE PURPOSE OF THIS LESSON?

The purpose of this teaching is simply to ever keep the symbol and concept of the "towel" before you. That is, the job of a preacher or teacher, in the church, is FIRST to serve; as Christ gave us the example of washing feet. So, the question before us now is, "ARE YOU INTO TITLES OR TOWELS?"

II.
SERVING IN ANOTHER MAN'S HOUSE

❊

DON'T JUST FOCUS
ON YOUR OWN PERSONAL VISION.

The focus in the body of Christ, for the last number of years (as of this writing), has been for you to fulfill the vision for YOUR life. While that is fundamentally a good message, it has been greatly abused. Therefore, you have many parts of the body of Christ fragmented and ineffective because many people are focused only on what they feel that they are called to do.

However, the Bible teaches us that our vision will be fulfilled when we give our all to fulfilling our leader's vision. Luke 16:12 **says,** *And if ye have not been faithful in that which is another man's, who shall give you that which is your own?* In other words, when you labor for another person to be promoted, God will assign someone to work for your promotion![59]

With this in mind, respect your leader, and never look to him/her as simply a tool to get you where you want to go in life. This writer has learned by experience that *respect will take you a long ways.* Whatever you respect moves toward you, and what-

---

59   hompson, Robb. Excellence in the Workplace. Family Harvest: Tinley Park, 2002.

ever you disrespect distances itself from you. Respect carries the meaning of, "holding others in high esteem or deeming others as distinguished and worthy." [60]

THREE EXAMPLES OF MEN WHO WERE NUMBER ONE AT BEING NUMBER TWO.

People often fail to realize that some of the greatest people in the Bible never had their own "house." But, they were faithful and fulfilled while serving under another person's leadership.

A.   Joseph. As great a leader as Joseph was, he never was the top man in command. The Pharaoh was ruler of Egypt and Joseph was faithful at being second in command, [39]And Pharaoh said unto Joseph, Forasmuch as God hath shewed thee all this, there is none so discreet and wise as thou art: [40]Thou shalt be over my house, and according unto thy word shall all my people be ruled: only in the throne will I be greater than thou (Genesis 41:39-40).

B.   Nehemiah. Nehemiah has gone down in biblical history as being the great leader who rebuilt the walls of Jerusalem, years after they had been destroyed by the Babylonians. However, Nehemiah was never the top man in charge; he had to answer to the king of Persia, [5]And I said unto the

---

60   Ibid.

king, If it please the king, and if thy servant have found favour in thy sight, that thou wouldest send me unto Judah, unto the city of my fathers' sepulchres, that I may build it. (Nehemiah 2:5).

C.   Stephen. Stephen was probably one of the most anointed men that ever lived. However, as far as church leadership is concerned, he never rose higher than the office of deacon. He did not attempt to give himself some type of extraordinary title (like "apostle" or "prophet"), but was simply content being an anointed deacon; for this was God's will for his life, 5And the saying pleased the whole multitude: and they chose Stephen, a man full of faith and of the Holy Ghost, and Philip, and Prochorus, and Nicanor, and Timon, and Parmenas, and Nicolas a proselyte of Antioch (Acts 6:5).

THE RULES OF THE HOUSE

If you are working in another man's house, you need to give him/her the same things that you would look for if it was your house. Again, what you make happen for someone else, God will make happen for you:

A.   **Complete and follow through on your assignments.** You are never rewarded for your intentions. You are only rewarded for your completions – the actions that push you toward excellence.[61]

B. **Stay committed through good and bad times.** Respect for your present assignment is proof that you are expecting a future reward.[62]

C. **Go above and beyond what is expected of you.** This will help you with being promoted in every area of life. Promotion is never granted from just doing what is assigned to you; that's why you must do more than what is expected of you (be willing to go the "extra mile" see Matthew 5:41).[63]

D. **Gain the reputation of being a low maintenance problem solver.** Leaders in every area of life will gravitate to the person who answers their most immediate need. You will be remembered for the problems you solve or the problems you create! [64]

E. **Remember that there is a difference between being a leader and a worker.** A worker says, "I'll get the job done," whereas a leader says, "I'll get some people together and we'll get the job done."[65]

---

61 Thompson, Robb. Excellence in the Workplace. Family Harvest: Tinley Park, 2002.

62 Ibid.

63 Ibid.

64 Ibid.

65 Cutshall, Bryan. "Twin Rivers Worship Center." Twin Rivers: Saint Louis, 2009.

F.   Don't get stagnant; continue to sharpen your skills.
Do this by:[66]

- Taking care of your personal appearance.

- Becoming an expert about your job.

- Giving attention to detail.

G.   Maintain your determination. You must do this even when you feel mistreated and unappreciated; stay focused on God's will for you. The mark of a true servant is that he/she has abandoned all personal pressures in order to become a tool in the hand of the One he/she serves.[67]

H.   Be consistent; avoid being shaky and moody. The test of a true servant is if you act like a servant even if you are treated like one.[68]

---

66 Thompson, Robb. Excellence in the Workplace. Family Harvest: Tinley Park, 2002.

67 Thompson, Robb. Excellence in the Workplace. Family Harvest: Tinley Park, 2002.

68 Ibid.

III.
THE CHARACTERISTICS OF A GODLY SERVANT

❀

WHY SHOULD THERE BE QUALIFICATIONS FOR PREACHERS AND TEACHERS?

A lot of times people in the church can be very "weird" and feel that they are to do something because they are led, or because they did it in the last church that they were a member of. However, any type of valid organization has prerequisites before you just jump and start doing a job.

As a preacher or teacher remember that Paul gave the following list of qualities a church leader should possess for two reasons, (1) to provide guidelines for churches to select leaders and, (2) to give church leaders a checkpoint for their own spiritual lives. The characteristics are as follows:[69]

1 Timothy 3:1-12 (The Message).[70] [1-7]If anyone wants to provide leadership in the church, good! But there are preconditions: A leader must be well-thought-of, committed to his wife, cool and collected, accessible, and hospitable. He must know

---

69 Maxwell, John. The Maxwell Leadership Bible. Nelson: Nashville, 2007.

70 Peterson, Eugene E. The Message. NAV: Colorado Springs, 2005.

what he's talking about, not be overfond of wine, not pushy but gentle, not thin-skinned, not money-hungry. He must handle his own affairs well, attentive to his own children and having their respect. For if someone is unable to handle his own affairs, how can he take care of God's church? He must not be a new believer, lest the position go to his head and the Devil trip him up. Outsiders must think well of him, or else the Devil will figure out a way to lure him into his trap. [8-13]The same goes for those who want to be servants in the church: serious, not deceitful, not too free with the bottle, not in it for what they can get out of it. They must be reverent before the mystery of the faith, not using their position to try to run things. Let them prove themselves first. If they show they can do it, take them on. No exceptions are to be made for women—same qualifications: serious, dependable, not sharp-tongued, not overfond of wine. Servants in the church are to be committed to their spouses, attentive to their own children, and diligent in looking after their own affairs. Those who do this servant work will come t*o be highly respected, a real credit to this Jesus-faith.*

DO YOU HAVE THE QUALITIES TO BE A LEADER IN THE CHURCH?

Based on the passage that we have just read from the Message Bible, ask yourself the following ten questions:[71]

---

71   Maxwell, John. The Maxwell Leadership Bible. Nelson: Nashville, 2007.

- Am I quick to improve those areas that can damage my integrity?

- Do I love my spouse as Christ loved the Church?

- Am I a master of myself, that I may be a servant to many?

- Do I exhibit a warm and welcoming spirit?

- Do I consistently help others learn and become better disciples?

- Am I sober, watchful, and diligent, so that I do not damage those who watch me?

- Do I have an approachable disposition that brings peace and healing?

- Am I allowing my leadership to be controlled by the rich?

- Do I manage my own family before I try to manage the church?

- Am I a seasoned, solid example for both insiders and outsiders?

SOME QUALITIES THAT PREACHERS AND TEACHERS SHOULD HAVE

In closing, if you are going to be a servant-leader, this writer feels that, along with the characteristics that are mentioned in the Bible, a good preacher or teacher must also have people skills; especially in dealing with God's people. Because you are dealing with the saints, there are two skills that you must master:

A. **The skill of tact.** A keen sense of what to do or say in order to maintain good relations with others or avoid offense.[72]

B. **The skill of diplomacy.** Skill in handling affairs without arousing hostility.[73]

SUMMARY

Through teaching on (1) servanthood, (2) being faithful in another man's house and (3) the characteristics of a godly leader, this lesson has kept the symbol and concept of the "towel" (or servanthood) before you. The job of a leader (preacher or teacher) in the church is to serve; this is why Christ gave us the example of washing feet. So, the question to take home and meditate on today is, "ARE YOU INTO TITLES OR TOWELS?

---

72 Mish, Frederick C. Webster's Ninth New Collegiate Dictionary. Webster: Springfield, 1989.

73 Mish, Frederick C. Webster's Ninth New Collegiate Dictionary. Webster: Springfield, 1989.

YOUR MESSAGE MUST EXALT CHRIST

❋

LESSON 6:

STAY WITH THE GOSPEL

"Let us draw near with a true heart in full assurance of faith, having our hearts sprinkled from an evil conscience, and our bodies washed with pure water."

- ROMANS 1:14-16 -

❋

LESSON 7:

YOU SHOULD HAVE A BASIC UNDERSTANDING OF THE GOSPEL

LESSON 6:

STAY WITH THE GOSPEL

*(Unless otherwise indicated all Scripture quotations are
from the King James Version of the Holy Bible)*

❋

CONTENTS:

WHAT IS THE GOSPEL

ROMANS: THE GOSPEL EXPLAINED

ONE GOSPEL FOR THE WHOLE WORLD

I.
WHAT IS THE GOSPEL?

❂

Romans 1:14-16. *[14]I am debtor both to the Greeks, and to the Barbarians; both to the wise, and to the unwise. [15]So, as much as in me is, I am ready to preach the gospel to you that are at Rome also. [16]For I am not ashamed of the gospel of Christ: for it is the power of God unto salvation to every one that believeth; to the Jew first, and also to the Greek.*

PURPOSE OF THIS LESSON

Since the rise of the information and technology age, many nations are now more open to new ideas, philosophies and religious teaching than in times past. Even the body of Christ has become infiltrated with various philosophies. However, this lesson is given simply to remind us that there is only one Gospel for everyone. Preachers and teachers should "stay with the Gospel," if souls are to be saved. And, it is only by repenting and believing in the Gospel of Jesus Christ that a person may obtain salvation and fellowship with God. We must strive to remind our listeners of this.

WHAT IS THE GOSPEL?

Gospel (from the Greek word *euangelion*) means, "Good News."[74] It is the good news or glad tidings of the kingdom of God and salvation through Jesus Christ's death, burial and resurrection.[75]

WHAT IS THE FULL GOSPEL?

As Pentecostals we believe in the "Full Gospel." The Full Gospel includes: the redeeming power of Jesus Christ for salvation because of Calvary, and the Baptism of the Holy Ghost for service and holy, victorious living because of Pentecost. [76] Our call is to preach Jesus Christ, God's Son: as the Savior, Baptizer with the Holy Ghost, Healer and soon coming King.[77]

BUT, IS THERE MORE THAN ONE GOSPEL?

There is only one Gospel for the whole world. But, in his day, Paul warned about counterfeit preaching and counterfeit

---

74 Strong, James. The Strongest Strong's. Zondervan: Grand Rapids, 2001.

75 Vine, W. E. Vine's Complete Expository Dictionary of Old and New Testament Words. Nelson: Nashville, 1996.

76 http://www.fullgospelbaptist.org/. (Accessed, February 11, 2011).

77 http://www.foursquare.org/about/our_purpose. (Accessed, February 11, 2011).

"Gospels." In other words this is preaching that tickles the ears, entertains and inspires; but does not have any power to save. Preachers and teachers, in regard to this Paul gave two warnings:

Galatians 1:6. I marvel that ye are so soon removed from him that called you into the grace of Christ unto another gospel:

Galatians 1:8. But though we, or an angel from heaven, preach any other gospel unto you than that which we have preached unto you, let him be accursed.

So, our exhortation today is not to be ashamed of the Old Fashioned Gospel that has power to save. This is the message of the book of Romans. Let's read on further and learn more about this powerful book.

II.

ROMANS: THE GOSPEL EXPLAINED

❂

THE PURPOSE OF ROMANS

Paul wrote Romans at the city of Corinth. Phoebe, a servant of the Lord, took it to Rome for Paul (Romans 16:1). Paul didn't start the church at Rome. Christianity was planted in Rome by some of those who had been at Jerusalem on the day of Pentecost (Acts 2:10).

The church at Rome was very large and was made up of Jews and Gentiles (or non-Jews). The church was so large that the Roman Christians had more than one place of meeting (Romans 16:14, 15).

Paul wrote to this church to explain to them the great doctrines of the Gospel. His letter was a "word in season," because it opened up in a clear and concise manner the whole system of the Gospel, in its relation both to Jew and Gentile. Both groups are justified by faith. There is no Jewish Gospel or Gentile Gospel; there is one Gospel for the whole world.[78] This is a great doctrinal truth for preachers and teachers both to remember and share with their listeners.

---

78 Easton, M. G. Illustrated Bible Dictionary, Third Edition. Nelson: Grand Rapids, 1897.

THE MESSAGE OF ROMANS

The ancient Israelites had a tremendous sin problem, which was displayed in their constant practice of idolatry. Idolatry was appealing to them because the big focus of idolatry was sex. There was no way that the Law, given by Moses, could help the people live better lives. God just about destroyed the nation, but all that produced was an outward change, very little inwardly. It was not until Jesus came and died for our sins that the Israelites (and now all humanity) has the ability to be free from the desire, practice and penalty of sin. This is the message of the book of Romans (see Romans 3:23; 6:23 and 10:9-10). There is good news for everyone! There is one Gospel for the whole world!

OUTLINE OF ROMANS

Again, the purpose of Romans is to explain the Gospel. If you understand this point, being able to outline the book becomes very simple:[79]

A.   Introduction: Romans 1:1-15.

B.   The Gospel Explained: Romans 1:16-8:39.

C.   The Gospel and the Nation of Israel: Romans 9-11.

---

79   Alexander, David, Ed. Eerdman's Handbook to the Bible. Eerdman's: Grand Rapids, 1973.

D. Living the Christian Life, because of the Gospel: Romans 12-15:13.

E. Closing: Romans 16.

Now, let's go further and understand our text and the fact that there is one Gospel for the whole world...

III.

ONE GOSPEL FOR THE WHOLE WORLD

❀

THE THREE "I AM STATEMENTS" OF PAUL

Again, Romans 1:14-17 is the primary Scripture of this entire letter (book) of Romans. In this passage Paul makes three striking statements that help to explain why there is only one Gospel for the whole world:

1.   I am debtor (Romans 1:14). Paul said that he was debtor (or obligated) both to the Greeks, and to the Barbarians; both to the wise, and to the unwise. This means that he was going to bring forward a charge of sinfulness against everyone, Jews and Gentiles (also see Romans 3:23). And, the ONLY method of deliverance from the penalty of sin (for everyone) is faith in the mercy of God, through Jesus Christ (see Romans 6:23).[80]

2.   I am ready to preach (Romans 1:15). The preaching of the Gospel was the very heartbeat of Paul's ministry. He had to preach.

---

80   [7] Henry, Matthew. Matthew Henry's Commentary on the Whole Bible: Complete and Un abridged in One Volume. Hendrickson: Peabody, 2008.

[8] http://en.wikipedia.org/wiki/Book_of_romans. (Accessed, February 11, 2011).

1 Corinthians 9:16 says, "For though I preach the gospel, I have nothing to glory of: for necessity is laid upon me; yea, woe is unto me, if I preach not the gospel!"

3. I am not ashamed (Romans 1:16). Why would there be any cause for shame of the Gospel? Paul said that he was not "ashamed" (epaiscúnomai) of the Gospel because it holds power (dúnamis). He was unashamed of his love for this Gospel that he preached about Jesus Christ. You see, people wanted to make Paul ashamed by spreading a rumor that he was going around downing the Jews. Paul knew this was not true. So, to strike back at his accusers, he said that this message of salvation was to "Jew first" and then to everyone else; one Gospel for the whole world.[81] All preachers and teachers should remember this vital truth!

81

LESSON 7:

YOU SHOULD HAVE A BASIC UNDERSTANDING OF SALVATION

(Unless otherwise indicated all Scripture quotations are from the King James Version of the Holy Bible)

❋

CONTENTS:

INTRODUCTION

WHAT SALVATION IS NOT

SAVED FROM WHAT?

CAN YOU LOSE YOUR SALVATION

MISCONCEPTIONS ABOUT HELL

I.

INTRODUCTION

*(Unless otherwise indicated all Scripture quotations
are from the King James Version of the Holy Bible)*

❀

PURPOSE OF THIS LESSON

This lesson was designed to give a very basic explanation of
the experience of salvation. This is important, because if you are going to preach and teach, with the purpose of people of being saved,
you yourself should understand salvation. This lesson will also answer some of the questions and distill some of the myths in regard
to salvation.

WHAT DO WE MEAN BY "SAVED?"

Every Christian does not use the term "saved" when it comes
to our relationship with God. Many denominations refer to being "converted" or "joining the Church," but seldom use the term
"saved." The majority of Christians, especially the Catholics, Orthodox and Anglicans rarely use "saved" as a part of their vocabulary.

It is important to note that mostly Pentecostals, Evangelicals or
Fundamentalists use the term "saved." Because our faith (the Church
Of God In Christ) falls into the Pentecostal category of Christianity;

this is why you hear the term "saved" and "salvation" used so much in our churches. The term saved is used quite a bit in the New Testament:

VOCABULARY WORDS

A.   Catholic.[82] The largest (1 billion people) Christian denomination and claims to be the oldest Christian denomination (2000 years old).

B.   Orthodox.[83] Second largest (300 million people) Christian denomination and also claims to be the oldest (2000 years old). Separated from the Catholic Church in 1054.

C.   Anglican.[84] Third largest (85 million people) Christian denomination. Even though this faith is 1,415 years old; it did not separate from the Catholic Church until 478 years ago.[85]

D.   Pentecostal.[86] A renewal movement within Christianity that places special emphasis on a direct personal experience of God through the baptism with the Holy Spirit.

---

82   "Number of Catholics on the Rise". Zenit News Agency. 27 April 2010. http://www.zenit.org/rssenglish-29058. Retrieved 2 May 2010.

83   http://christianity.about.com/od/easternorthodoxy/p/orthodoxprofile.htm. (Accessed, September 29, 2012)

84   "The Anglican Communion Official website - Provincial Registry". Anglicancommunion.org. http://www.anglicancommunion.org/tour/index.cfm. Retrieved 2012-07-20.

85   The English Reformation by Professor Andrew Pettegree. Bbc.co.uk.

86   "Spirit and Power: A 10-Country Survey of Pentecostals", Executive Summary. The Pew Forum on Religion and Public Life.

E. Evangelical.[87] Evangelicalism de-emphasizes ritual and emphasizes the devotion of the individual, requiring him or her to meet certain active commitments, including:

- The need for personal conversion, or being "born again."

- A high regard for biblical authority.

- An emphasis on teachings that proclaim the saving death and resurrection of the Son of God, Jesus Christ.

- Actively expressing and sharing the Gospel.

F. Fundamentalism. A movement within Christianity upholding a literal reading of the Bible or official teachings of the Church.[88] [89] Several core beliefs include:[90]

- The inerrancy of the Bible.

- The literal nature of the Biblical accounts, especially regarding Christ's miracles and the Creation account in Genesis.

- The Virgin Birth of Christ.

---

87 "Defining Evangelicalism". Institute for the Study of American Evangelicals, Wheaton College. http://isae.wheaton.edu/defining-evangelicalism/. Retrieved August 31, 2011.

88 Richard P. McBrien. The HarperCollins Encyclopedia of Catholicism. HarperCollins.

89 Brennan Hill, Paul F. Knitter, William Madges. Faith, Religion & Theology: A Contemporary Introduction. Twenty-Third Publications.

90 http://www.webcitation.org/query?url=http://www.geocities.com/Athens/Parthenon/6528/ fundcont.htm&date=2009-10-25+06:18:43. (Accessed, September 29, 2012).

- The bodily resurrection and physical return of Christ.

- The substitutionary atonement of Christ on the Cross.

SOME SCRIPTURE REFERENCES
FOR THE WORD "SAVED."

A.   Matthew 1:21 (New King James Version NKJV).[91] And she will bring forth a Son, and you shall call His name JESUS, for He will <u>save</u> His people from their sins."

B.   Acts 16:29-31 (New King James Version (NKJV).[92] [29]Then he called for a light, ran in, and fell down trembling before Paul and Silas. [30]And he brought them out and said, "Sirs, what must I do to be <u>saved?"</u> [31]So they said, "Believe on the Lord Jesus Christ, and you will be <u>saved,</u> you and your household."

C.   Romans 10:9-10 (New King James Version NKJV).[93] That if you confess with your mouth the Lord Jesus and believe in your heart that God has raised Him from the dead, you will be saved. [10]For with the heart one believes unto righteousness, and with the mouth confession is made unto salvation.

---

91   Holy Bible. The Open Bible New King James Version. Nelson: Nashville, 2008.

92   Ibid.

93   Ibid.

II.

WHAT SALVATION IS NOT

✦

A.   Salvation is not doing good deeds.
Isaiah 64:6 (New Living Translation NLT).[94] We
are all infected and impure with sin. When we
display <u>our righteous deeds, they are nothing but
filthy rags.</u> Like autumn leaves, we wither and fall,
and our sins sweep us away like the wind.

B.   Salvation is not just being a good person.
Ephesians 2:8-9 (New Living Translation
(NLT).[95] [8] God saved you by his grace when you believed. And <u>you can't take credit for this; it is a gift
from God.</u> [9] Salvation is not a reward for the good
things we have done, so none of us can boast about
it.

C.   Salvation is not just abstaining from doing wrong.
2 Timothy 3:5 (Contemporary English Version
CEV).[96] Even though they will make a <u>show of being religious,</u> their religion won't be real. Don't
have anything to do with such people.

---

94   Holy Bible. New Living Translation. Tyndale: Carol Stream, 2004.

95   Ibid.

96   Holy Bible. Contemporary English Version. ABS: New York, 1995.

D.   Salvation is not earned.

Romans 5:15 (New Living Translation NLT).[97] But there is a great difference between Adam's sin and God's gracious gift. For the sin of this one man, Adam, brought death to many. But even greater is <u>God's wonderful grace and his gift of forgiveness</u> to many through this other man, Jesus Christ.

E.   Salvation is not church membership.

1 John 2:19 (Contemporary English Version CEV).[98] These people came from our own group, <u>yet they were not part of us.</u> If they had been part of us, they would have stayed with us. But they left, which proves that they did not belong to our group.

F.   Salvation is not just choosing Christianity as your religion.

James 1:27 (New King James Version NKJV).[99] <u>Pure and undefiled religion</u> before God and the Father is this: to visit orphans and widows in their trouble, and to keep oneself unspotted from the world.

G.   Salvation is not attending church.

Mark 7:6 (Contemporary English Version (CEV). [6] Jesus replied: You are nothing but show-offs! The

---

97 Holy Bible. New Living Translation. Tyndale: Carol Stream, 2004.

98 Holy Bible. Contemporary English Version. ABS: New York, 1995.

99 Holy Bible. The Open Bible New King James Version. Nelson: Nashville, 2008.

prophet Isaiah was right when he wrote that God had said, "All of you praise me with your words, but you never really think about me."

III.

SAVED FROM WHAT?

❀

HERE IS WHAT WE ARE SAVED FROM:

A.   **We are saved from our sins.**

John 1:29.[100] The next day John saw Jesus coming toward him, and said, "Behold! The Lamb of God who <u>takes away the sin of the world!</u>

B.   **We are saved from the consequence of sin.**

John 5:24.[101] "Most assuredly, I say to you, he who hears My word and believes in Him who sent Me has everlasting life, and <u>shall not come into judgment, but has passed from death into life.</u>

C.   **We are saved from eternal damnation.**

Romans 5:9.[102] Much more then, having now been justified by His blood, <u>we shall be saved from wrath</u> through Him.

---

100   Holy Bible. The Open Bible New King James Version. Nelson: Nashville, 2008.

101   Ibid.

102   Ibid.

D.   We are saved from separation from God.

Hebrews 10:19.[103] Therefore, brethren, having <u>boldness to enter the Holiest by the blood </u>of Jesus,

What do people mean when they say there are, "saved, sanctified and filled with the precious gift of the Holy Ghost and that with a mighty burning fire" and they "do speak in tongues as the Spirit gives utterance?"

A.   Saved means: free from sin (wrong doing, thinking and living), guilt and all of sins and penalties (which is death and eternal judgment).

B.   Sanctified means: the God-given ability to live a holy (clean, pure) life, without sin (wrong doing, thinking and living).

C.   Filled with the precious gift of the Holy Ghost means: having God's power, authorization and ability to represent Him in this world.

D.   With a mighty burning fire means: God's Spirit keeps us pure and devoted to Him.

E.   Speaking in tongues as the spirit gives utterance means: to supernaturally speak a language that you have never learned before. Your tongue is your most "out of control" part of your body. Speaking languages supernaturally is not only a sign that God is in control of your life; but it is the Spirit of God praying through you.

---

103   Ibid.

Does it matter what type of church you go to?

According to the Bible it does. We are saved by the truth of God's Word. If a church is not preaching the truth of the Bible; people CANNOT be saved:

A.   Truth is found in the Bible.

John 17:17. Sanctify them through thy truth: thy word is truth.

B.   Truth makes us free.

John 8:32. And ye shall know the truth, and the truth shall make you free.

C.   Truth is in Jesus.

Ephesians 4:21. If so be that ye have heard him, and have been taught by him, as the truth is in Jesus:

D.   To know the truth (1) you have to study (2) you have to rely on the Holy Ghost to bear witness that something you hear is right or not.

John 16:13. Howbeit when he, the Spirit of truth, is come, he will guide you into all truth: for he shall not speak of himself; but whatsoever he shall hear, that shall he speak: and he will shew you things to come.

CAN PEOPLE OF OTHER RELIGIONS BE SAVED?

Most any religion accepts and honors Jesus as a good man, teacher and prophet. However, to experience salvation, a person must believe the following truths. Most religions do not accept these truths about Jesus. Therefore, salvation can only be found in Him and through the Church which He established:

A.   **Jesus is the Son of God.**
      John 3:16. For God so loved the world, that he gave his <u>only begotten Son,</u> that whosoever believeth in him should not perish, but have everlasting life.

B.   **Jesus is the only way to salvation.**
      John 14:6. Jesus saith unto him, I am the way, the truth, and the life: no man cometh unto the Father, but by me.

ISN'T A SAVED LIFE A DULL AND BORING LIFE?

Not at all, "For the kingdom of God is not meat and drink; but righteousness, and peace, and joy in the Holy Ghost" (Romans 14:17).

IV.

CAN YOU LOSE
YOUR SALVATION?

❀

DO YOU HAVE TO GET SAVED ALL OVER AGAIN,
EVERY TIME YOU SIN OR DO WRONG?

While we (in the Church Of God In Christ) do not believe
in the teaching of "eternal security," "once in Christ, never out,"
or "once saved, always saved," it would be absurd to believe that
a person gets saved, backslides and gets saved over again all day
long. A person is either saved or not (not in and out). Consider
the following points:

A.   A true Christian will not practice sin.

1 John 3:4-10 (Contemporary English Version
CEV).[104] 4 Everyone who sins breaks God's law,
because sin is the same as breaking God's law. 5 You
know that Christ came to take away sins. He isn't
sinful, 6 and people who stay one in their hearts
with him won't keep on sinning. If they do keep
on sinning, they don't know Christ, and they have

---

104   Holy Bible. Contemporary English Version. ABS: New York, 1995.

never seen him.[7] Children, don't be fooled. Anyone who does right is good, just like Christ himself. [8] Anyone who keeps on sinning belongs to the devil. He has sinned from the beginning, but the Son of God came to destroy all that he has done. [9] God's children cannot keep on being sinful. His life-giving power lives in them and makes them his children, so that they cannot keep on sinning. [10] You can tell God's children from the Devil's children, because those who belong to the Devil refuse to do right or to love each other.

B.   If you, a Christian sins, you confess it, not get saved all over again.

1 John 1:8-10; 2:1-2. (Contemporary English Version CEV).[105] [8] If we say that we have not sinned, we are fooling ourselves, and the truth isn't in our hearts. [9] But if we confess our sins to God, he can always be trusted to forgive us and take our sins away. [10] If we say that we have not sinned, we make God a liar, and his message isn't in our hearts. 1 My children, I am writing this so that you won't sin. But if you do sin, Jesus Christ always does the right thing, and he will speak to the Father for us. [2] Christ is the sacrifice that takes away our sins and the sins of all the world's people.

---

105   Holy Bible. Contemporary English Version. ABS: New York, 1995.

C. Known, non-confessed sin will cause your soul to be lost.

Revelation 22:11-12 (Contemporary English Version CEV).[106] [11] Evil people will keep on being evil, and everyone who is dirty-minded will still be dirty-minded. But good people will keep on doing right, and God's people will always be holy. [12] Then I was told: I am coming soon! And when I come, I will reward everyone for what they have done.

---

106 Ibid.

V.
MISCONCEPTIONS ABOUT HELL

❀

A. People who never heard the Gospel are YET subject to end up in Hell.

> **Romans 2:12-16** (Contemporary English Version CEV).[107] [12] Those people who don't know about God's Law will still be punished for what they do wrong. And the Law will be used to judge everyone who knows what it says. [13] God accepts those who obey his Law, but not those who simply hear it. [14] Some people naturally obey the Law's commands, even though they don't have the Law. [15] This proves that the conscience is like a law written in the human heart. And it will show whether we are forgiven or condemned, [16] when God appoints Jesus Christ to judge everyone's secret thoughts, just as my message says.

B. The Devil, as far as we know, has never been to Hell. So it is an untruth when you hear people say that when Jesus died, He went down to Hell and while there he was taunted by the Devil and demons.

---

107   Holy Bible. Contemporary English Version. ABS: New York, 1995.

Ephesians 2:2 (Contemporary English Version CEV).[108] You followed the ways of this world and obeyed the Devil. He rules the world, and his spirit has power over everyone who doesn't obey God.

C. **The Devil and his demons are not the leaders of Hell.**

Matthew 25:41 (Contemporary English Version CEV).[109] Then the king will say to those on his left, "Get away from me! You are under God's curse. Go into the everlasting fire prepared for the devil and his angels!

D. **The devil and his demons will not be tormenting people forever in Hell.**

Revelation 20:10. And the devil that deceived them was cast into the lake of fire and brimstone, where the beast and the false prophet are, and shall be tormented day and night for ever and ever.

E. **Hell is not a physical place; it is an unseen spiritual place.**

Ephesians 6:12. For we wrestle not against flesh and blood, but against principalities, against powers, against the rulers of the darkness of this world, against spiritual wickedness in high places.

---

108   Ibid.

109   Holy Bible. Contemporary English Version. ABS: New York, 1995.

How To Teach Effectively

❋

LESSON 8:

THE RESPONSIBILITY OF BIBLE TEACHER

"And he gave some, apostles; and some, prophets; and some, evangelists; and some, pastors and teachers; ¹² For the perfecting of the saints, for the work of the ministry, for the edifying of the body of Christ: ..."

- EPHESIANS 4:11-16 -

❋

LESSON 9:

HOW TO BE EFFECTIVE AT TEACHING THE BIBLE

"Go ye therefore, and teach all nations, baptizing them in the name of the Father, and of the Son, and of the Holy Ghost:..."

- MATTHEW 28:19-20 -

LESSON 8:

THE RESPONSIBILITY OF A BIBLE TEACHER

(Unless otherwise indicated all Scripture quotations are

from the King James Version of the Holy Bible)

❁

CONTENTS:

INTRODUCTION

HOW TO BE AND REMAIN
ANOINTED AS A BIBLE TEACHER

THE PRPOSE OF A BIBLE TEACHERS IS
TO HELP THE BODY OF CHRIST MATURE

TIPS FOR GROWING YOUR BIBLE CLASS

I.

INTRODUCTION

*(Unless otherwise indicated all Scripture quotations are
from the King James Version of the Holy Bible).*

❀

Ephesians 4:11-16. *[11] And he gave some, apostles; and some,
prophets; and some, evangelists; and some, pastors and teachers; [12] For
the perfecting of the saints, for the work of the ministry, for the edifying
of the body of Christ: [13] Till we all come in the unity of the faith, and of
the knowledge of the Son of God, unto a perfect man, unto the measure
of the stature of the fulness of Christ: [14] That we henceforth be no more
children, tossed to and fro, and carried about with every wind of doctrine, by the sleight of men, and cunning craftiness, whereby they lie in
wait to deceive; [15] But speaking the truth in love, may grow up into him in
all things, which is the head, even Christ: [16] From whom the whole body
fitly joined together and compacted by that which every joint supplieth,
according to the effectual working in the measure of every part, maketh
increase of the body unto the edifying of itself in love.*

BETTER GET SERIOUS!!!

Our text today, in Ephesians 4:11, describes an office known
as "pastor-teacher."[110] It's really one office, because those who are
pastors will naturally provide teaching from the Scriptures. That

---

110   Hoerber, Robert G. Concordia Self-Study Bible. Concordia: St. Louis, 1986.

is an awesome responsibility upon the pastor. Bible teachers are really in place to assist the pastor in providing quality Christian education, training and teaching to the people of God.[111] YOU CAN'T PLAY WITH THAT TYPE OF RESPONSIBILITY. With that in mind, it is totally unacceptable for teachers to:

• Skip class without notice.
• Consistently arrive after time for class to start.
• Have a nonchalant attitude.
• Fail to live a consistent Christian life.

---

111   Clarke, W. K. Concise Bible Commentary. MacMillan: New York, 1953.

II.

HOW TO BE AND REMAIN ANOINTED AS A BIBLE TEACHER

❋

A "SUPERNATURAL" CHURCH

Many years ago, Ephesus was a pretty important city. But, because there was so much opposition and witchcraft prevalent in the city of Ephesus (see Acts 19:19), God had to do some mighty miracles through Paul in order to get the people's attention (God's power, not your Bible knowledge, will win T.H.E.M. to Christ):

Acts 19:1-12 (Contemporary English Version CEV).[112]
1 While Apollos was in Corinth, Paul traveled across the hill country to Ephesus, where he met some of the Lord's followers. ² He asked them, "When you put your faith in Jesus, were you given the Holy Spirit?" "No!" they answered. "We have never even heard of the Holy Spirit."³ "Then why were you baptized?" Paul asked. They answered, "Because of what John taught." ⁴ Paul replied, "John baptized people so that they would turn to God. But he also told them that someone else was coming, and that they should put their faith in him.

---

112   Holy Bible. Contemporary English Version. ABS: New York, 1995.

Jesus is the one that John was talking about." [5] After the people heard Paul say this, they were baptized in the name of the Lord Jesus. [6] Then Paul placed his hands on them. The Holy Spirit was given to them, and they spoke unknown languages and prophesied. *[7] There were about twelve men in this group. [8] For three months Paul went to the Jewish meeting place and talked bravely with the people about God's kingdom. He tried to win them over, [9] but some of them were stubborn and refused to believe. In front of everyone they said terrible things about God's Way. Paul left and took the followers with him to the lecture hall of Tyrannus. He spoke there every day [10] for two years, until every Jew and Gentile in Asia had heard the Lord's message. [11]* God gave Paul the power to work great miracles. *[12] People even took handkerchiefs and aprons that had touched Paul's body, and they carried them to everyone who was sick. All of the sick people were healed, and the evil spirits went out.*

TO REACH PEOPLE, YOU MUST HAVE GOD'S POWER

This lets us know that it's important that we have the power of God to turn people's attention toward the Word of God. Listen to what Paul says about "head knowledge" of the Bible, but no power with God:

2 Corinthians 3:4-6 *(The Message (MSG).*[113] *4-6 We couldn't be more sure of ourselves in this—that you, written by Christ himself for God, are our letter of recommendation. We wouldn't think of writing this kind of letter about ourselves. Only God can write such a letter. His letter authorizes us to help carry out this new plan of action. The plan wasn't written out with ink on paper, with pages and pages of legal footnotes, killing your spirit. It's written with Spirit on spirit, his life on our lives!*

HOW DOES A TEACHER RECEIVE THIS EMPOWERMENT?

The Word says in Zechariah 4:6, "Then he answered and spake unto me, saying, This is the word of the LORD unto Zerubbabel, saying, Not by might, nor by power, but by my spirit, saith the LORD of hosts." You need the power of God because teaching is not about you, it's about the people. So, how do you receive the power of God (or the anointing)?

1.   **You must seek God to be filled with the Holy Ghost.**
        Luke 24:49. And, behold, I send the promise of my Father upon you: but tarry ye in the city of Jerusalem, until ye be endued with power from on high.

---

113   Peterson, Eugene E. The Message. NAV: Colorado Springs, 2005.

2.   Once filled, you must develop a worship, prayer and study life. Again, DO NOT JUST STUDY AND PRAY WHEN IT'S YOUR TIME TO TEACH. You should have a spiritual "reservoir" built up, so that when it's time to teach, you can do so from your "overflow" and not your "reservoir."

Luke 6:12. And it came to pass in those days, that he went out into a mountain to pray, and continued all night in prayer to God.

Ephesians 5:18. And be not drunk with wine, wherein is excess; but be filled with the Spirit;

3.   You must ask God to anoint you, believe that He has answered the prayer and in expectancy look for Him to administer the results.

Acts 4:24-31. 24 And when they heard that, they lifted up their voice to God with one accord, and said, Lord, thou art God, which hast made heaven, and earth, and the sea, and all that in them is: 25 Who by the mouth of thy servant David hast said, Why did the heathen rage, and the people imagine vain things? 26 The kings of the earth stood up, and the rulers were gathered together against the Lord, and against his Christ. 27 For of a truth against thy holy child Jesus, whom thou hast anointed, both Herod, and Pontius Pilate, with the Gentiles, and the people of Israel, were gathered together, 28 For to do whatsoever thy hand and thy counsel determined before to be done. ²⁹ And now, Lord, behold their threatenings: and grant unto thy servants, that with all boldness they may speak thy word, ³⁰ By stretching forth thine hand to heal; and that signs and wonders may be done by the name of thy holy child Jesus. ³¹ And when they had prayed, the place was shaken where they were assembled together; and they were all filled with the Holy Ghost, and they spake the word of God with boldness.

4.   You should ask other people to intercede for you, for your class, department or whatever area of ministry that you are involved in.

2 Thessalonians 3:1. Finally, brethren, pray for us, that the word of the Lord may have free course, and be glorified, even as it is with you:

5.   You have to constantly guard your heart and check your motives.

Proverbs 4:23. Keep thy heart with all diligence; for out of it are the issues of life.

III.

THE PURPOSE OF A BIBLE TEACHER IS TO HELP THE BODY OF CHRIST TO MATURE

❊

EPHESIANS IS ABOUT HIM IN THE PEOPLE

Ephesians is a long letter that was written by the Apostle Paul, to the church at Ephesus, while he was in prison. This is one of the few New Testament letters that is NOT addressing a problem in the church.[114] It actually was written to show the people of God who they are in Christ. Some form of "in Christ" is found many times throughout the book.[115]

GOD'S PEOPLE GROWING UP IN HIM.

Paul was always concerned that his church members would live what they were taught and not just accumulate a lot of biblical facts and figures. In Chapter 4 of Ephesians he stressed the need for the church people to practice what they have been taught.

---

114   Alexander, David. Eerdman's Handbook to the Bible. Eerdman's: Grand Rapids, 1973.

115   Bell, James Stuart and Stan Campbell. The Complete Idiot's Guide to the Bible. Penguin: New York, 2005.

Ephesians 4:1 (Amplified Bible AMP)[116] says, "I therefore, the prisoner for the Lord, appeal to and beg you to walk (lead a life) worthy of the [divine] calling to which you have been called [with behavior that is a credit to the summons to God's service." So, let's outline this chapter and see how it applies to Bible teachers benefiting the people:

1. The church should live up to its name (Ephesians 4:1-6). Unity is a sign that the church is living up to its calling to be the church.

2. Ministry gifts were given to mature the church (Ephesians 4:7-16). Listed in the ministry gifts section is the office known as Pastor-Teacher. Allow me to reiterate what I mentioned in Lesson 1:

    I strongly believe that there is a difference between having a talent to teach (for example, a school teacher), having a gift to teach (supernatural ability from God that may or may not manifest on a consistent basis) and having the office of teacher (which is generally tied to the pastoral office as "pastor-teacher"). See Romans 12:7 and Ephesians 4:11.

    While a Bible teacher may not be the pastor-teacher, think about it, THE PASTOR HAS GIVEN YOU THE PRIVILEGE TO USE YOUR GIFT AND TALENT TO HELP FEED GOD'S "FLOCK" WITH THE WORD OF GOD!!!!! FOR

---

116   Holy Bible. Amplified Version. Zondervan: Grand Rapids, 1987.

PEACE'S SAKE; PLEASE DO NOT EVER TAKE THAT
RESPONSIBILITY AND PRIVILEGE LIGHTLY!!!!!!!!!!!

3.   The church should live a Christian life (Ephesians 4:17-32).
Sometimes teachers may complain that there is little interest
in his/her class. However, people are much more critical in
this day and time; than they were years ago. PEOPLE ARE
WATCHING YOUR LIFE. Yes, you may be saved, sanctified
and filled with the Holy Ghost. But, believe it or not, it goes
beyond that. People are watching attitudes, inconsistencies,
double standards, etc. Many times this will cause people not
to "support" you. So, in this section of Ephesians Paul lists
some traits that it would be good for teachers to adopt. Think
about it; how can you help to mature the body of Christ as a
Bible teacher, if you are immature yourself?[117] So let's follow
what the Word of God says:

Ephesians 4:17-32 (New Living Translation NLT)[118] [17]
With the Lord's authority I say this: Live no longer as the
Gentiles do, for they are hopelessly confused. [18] Their minds
are full of darkness; they wander far from the life God gives
because they have closed their minds and hardened their
hearts against him. [19] They have no sense of shame. They
live for lustful pleasure and eagerly practice every kind of
impurity. [20] But that isn't what you learned about Christ. [21]
Since you have heard about Jesus and have learned the truth

---

117   Dake, Finnis Jennings. Dake's Annotated Reference Bible. Lawrenceville: Dake, 2001.

118   Holy Bible. New Living Translation. Tyndale: Carol Stream, 2004.

that comes from him, [22] throw off your old sinful nature and your former way of life, which is corrupted by lust and deception. [23] Instead, let the Spirit renew your thoughts and attitudes. [24] Put on your new nature, created to be like God— truly righteous and holy. [25] So stop telling lies. Let us tell our neighbors the truth, for we are all parts of the same body. [26] And "don't sin by letting anger control you." Don't let the sun go down while you are still angry, [27] for anger gives a foothold to the Devil. [28] If you are a thief, quit stealing. Instead, use your hands for good hard work, and then give generously to others in need. [29] Don't use foul or abusive language. Let everything you say be good and helpful, so that your words will be an encouragement to those who hear them. [30] And do not bring sorrow to God's Holy Spirit by the way you live. Remember, he has identified you as his own, guaranteeing that you will be saved on the day of redemption. [31] Get rid of all bitterness, rage, anger, harsh words, and slander, as well as all types of evil behavior. [32] Instead, be kind to each other, tenderhearted, forgiving one another, just as God through Christ has forgiven you.

IV.

TIPS FOR GROWING YOUR BIBLE CLASS

✵

A. **Keep a roster of your students.** Use this to make calls to remind students to be to class "bright and early."

B. **Remember special days.** A lot of times a church may be too large and busy to remember birthdays, anniversaries, etc. Bible classes are small enough to share in those special days. If your class does not have a budget, purchasing some inexpensive cards from the store is worth the investment.

C. **Use visual aids.** Everyone is not a "book learner." Use handouts, maps, power points presentations or whatever enhances peoples' ability to "experience" the text.

D. **Watch the "runaway train."** This is a class that has gone so far off of the subject that you don't even remember what the initial subject was. Every so often relate how the discussion pertains to the topic at hand and graciously and discreetly get the "train back on the track."

E. **Stay in your lane.** Stay in harmony with what your pastor teaches. Do not use your class to push your agenda or focus on "what's wrong with the church." God is watching and you reap what you sow. In other words, "What goes around, comes around."

F.   People love food. Inexpensive treats such as coffee and donuts go a long way.

G.   Provide incentives. Give out prizes for correct answers and following through on assignments.

H.   Make learning fun. Get to your class on time. Be enthused about the lesson. Provide attention grasping stories. DO NOT ACT LIKE YOU JUST WOKE UP Five MINUTES AGO AND REALLY DO NOT WANT TO BE THERE. As they say in the job market, "leave your feelings at the door." Strive to be a teacher like Jesus:

Mark 1:22. And they were astonished at his doctrine: for he taught them as one that had authority, and not as the scribes.

Mark 12:37. David therefore himself calleth him Lord; and whence is he then his son? And the common people heard him gladly.

LESSON 9:

HOW TO BE EFFECTIVE AT TEACHING THE BIBLE

(Unless otherwise indicated all Scripture quotations are from the King James Version of the Holy Bible)

❊

CONTENTS:

INTRODUCTION

REMINDERS TO PREACHERS AND TEACHERS

THE MIINSTRY OF TEACHING IN THE BOOK OF MATTHEW

TIPS ON BEING AN EFFECTIVE BIBLE TEACHER

I.

INTRODUCTION

(Unless otherwise indicated all Scripture quotations are
from the King James Version of the Holy Bible).

❁

Matthew 28:19-20. *[19] Go ye therefore, and teach all nations, baptizing them in the name of the Father, and of the Son, and of the Holy Ghost: [20] Teaching them to observe all things whatsoever I have commanded you: and, lo, I am with you always, even unto the end of the world. Amen.*

PURPOSE OF THIS LESSON.

To remind you, as a teacher, that it's all about the people. Whether you are a teacher, or minister in some other area, the purpose is to benefit the people by: teaching, evangelizing and motivating.

Bible classes especially should not just be a time of indoctrination, or arguing irrelevant facts that do not benefit the listener. People are looking for something practical when they attend church. Therefore, to properly train people how to live for God, our teaching must be practical, down to Earth, "how to," that lets people know that God is real and His Word is meant to be applied to everyday life and prepare us for the life to come.[119]

---

119   Murren, Doug. The Baby Boomerang. Regal: Ventura, 1990.

THE MANDATE TO THE APOSTLES HAS BEEN PASSED ON TO YOU!

In the text Jesus told his disciples to go and make disciples of all nations and to teach the people. This ministry of teaching has been passed down to you, because Jesus said (in the text), "teaching them to observe all things whatsoever I have commanded you." What an awesome privilege to carry on the ministry that Jesus started and passed on to the apostles! Once you realize the weight of this responsibility, you'll never look at the ministry of teaching the same way again.

II.

REMINDERS TO PREACHERS AND TEACHERS

❖

THE THREE "B'S"

A. **Be anointed.** All teachers should be anointed because they are teaching God's Word! This writer strongly believes that there is a difference between having a talent to teach (for example, a school teacher), having a gift to teach (supernatural ability from God that may or may not manifest on a consistent basis), and having the office of teacher (which is generally tied to the pastoral office as "pastor-teacher"). See Romans 12:7 and Ephesians 4:11. However, whatever category you fit in, you should learn to flow in the anointing to be effective.

B. Be clear on the basics. Sometimes we lose our students trying to be so "deep." Yes, the Bible tells us to move on from the basics, however, the average Christian appears now to not know the basics!!! So we must walk them through, step by step. The basics are found in:

Hebrews 6:1-2 (Contemporary English Version CEV).[120] We must try to become mature and start thinking about more than just the basic things we were taught about Christ. We shouldn't need to keep talking about why we ought to turn from deeds that bring death and why we ought to have faith in God. [2] And we shouldn't need to keep teaching about baptisms or about the laying on of hands or about people being raised from death and the future judgment.

C.   **Be a tour guide not a travel agent.** A travel agent can tell you about nice places, but may have never been there. A tour guide takes you to the destination and leads you through it, step by step.[121] God wants Bible teachers to be tour guides and not travel agents. In other words you must lead people through this Christian walk and not merely tell them about it. To make it plain, you must be an example.

---

120   Holy Bible. Contemporary English Version. ABS: New York, 1995.

121   Source unknown.

III.

THE MINISTRY OF TEACHING IN THE BOOK OF MATTHEW

❖

THE PURPOSE OF THE BOOK OF MATTHEW

Matthew is the most "Jewish" of the four Gospels. Matthew was a Jew writing to Jews. His aim was to prove to the Jewish people that not only is this their long awaited Savior; but this is also their king.

Kings are not known for their actions; they have plenty of subjects to act on their behalf. Kings are known for the words that proceed from their mouth. The reason is because their word is law! No such thing as a legislative branch. A King is the legislative executive and judicial branches all in one:

> *Isaiah 33:22. For the LORD is our judge, the LORD is our lawgiver, the LORD is our king; he will save us.*

Therefore, in Matthew you find more of what Jesus said than in any of the other four Gospels. Knowing what Jesus said is very important to the ministry of teaching and training believers on how to grow in their faith.

NOT A GREAT "SUGGESTION" AT ALL!

Our text is commonly known as the "Great Commission." This is where Jesus sends His disciples out into the world to evangelize. This was NOT A SUGGESTION, but a command! Matthew 28:19-20 shares THREE ACTION WORDS for those who wish to become disciples:

A.   **GOING.** Teachers must realize that it is our responsibility to be proactive toward the spiritual progress of our students. We are not merely "waiting" for them to show up; but actually taking part and providing accountability in their walk with Christ.

B.   **BAPTIZING.** Our efforts as teachers must be evangelistic. We can never assume that everyone within the confines of our classes is saved or even understands the plan of salvation. Much like a clear presentation of the Gospel, an invitation needs to be provided in a worship service; the plan of salvation should also be presented in biblical classes.

C.   **TEACHING.** To teach is to provide clear EXPLANATION of the Word of God and training to cause the Christian to grow in Christ; teaching is not just INFORMATION or INSPIRATION.

MATTHEW'S VERSION OF THE GREAT COMMISSION.

Take note that Matthew's account of the commission is totally different from Mark, Luke-Acts and John:

- Mark focuses on **PREACHING.**

    Mark 16:15. [15] And he said unto them, Go ye into all the world, and preach the gospel to every creature.

- Luke-Acts focuses on **PREACHING AND WITNESSING.**
    Luke 24:47-48. [47] And that repentance and remission of sins should be preached in his name among all nations, beginning at Jerusalem. [48] And ye are witnesses of these things.

    Acts 1:8. But ye shall receive power, after that the Holy Ghost is come upon you: and ye shall be witnesses unto me both in Jerusalem, and in all Judaea, and in Samaria, and unto the uttermost part of the earth.

- John focuses on **FEEDING THE "SHEEP."**
    John 21:15-17. [15] So when they had dined, Jesus saith to Simon Peter, Simon, son of Jonas, lovest thou me more than these? He saith unto him, Yea, Lord; thou knowest that I love thee. He saith unto him, Feed my lambs. [16] He saith to him again the second time, Simon, [son] of Jonas, lovest thou me? He saith unto him, Yea, Lord; thou knowest that I love thee. He saith unto him, Feed my sheep. [17] He saith unto him the third time, Simon, [son] of Jonas, lovest thou me? Peter was grieved because he said unto him the third time, Lovest thou me? And he said unto

him, Lord, thou knowest all things; thou knowest that I love thee. Jesus saith unto him, Feed my sheep.

However, Matthew's emphasis is on the ministry of TEACHING, "Go ye therefore and TEACH..." But, what does it mean to teach? It means to make disciples. A disciple is a learner, follower or imitator of Christ. This is our goal as teachers - to benefit our students, by instructing them in the Word of God, so that the student may be more like Christ. (Note: discipling or teaching are totally different from indoctrination or simply perusing biblical facts and data). Consider our text in a few different versions:

Matthew 28:19 (Contemporary English Version CEV).[122] Go to the people of all nations and make them my disciples. Baptize them in the name of the Father, the Son, and the Holy Spirit,

Matthew 28:19 (The Message MSG).[123] Jesus, undeterred, went right ahead and gave his charge: "God authorized and commanded me to commission you: Go out and train everyone you meet, far and near, in this way of life, marking them by baptism in the threefold name: Father, Son, and Holy Spirit.

---

122   Holy Bible. Contemporary English Version. ABS: New York, 1995.

123   Peterson, Eugene E. The Message. NAV: Colorado Springs, 2005.

IV.

TIPS ON BEING AN EFFECTIVE BIBLE TEACHER

❁

If people are going to grow from the teaching of the Word of God then our teaching and methods must be "cutting edge." Think about it, lives were changed through Jesus' ministry because He is an excellent communicator:

Matthew 7:28-29 (New Living Translation). [124] 28 When Jesus had finished saying these things, the crowds were amazed at his teaching, 29 for he taught with real authority—quite unlike their teachers of religious law.

Mark 12:37 (Contemporary English Version). [125] If David called the Messiah his Lord, how can the Messiah be his son?" The large crowd enjoyed listening to Jesus teach.

While we may all have different methods of delivery, teaching and communicating, the following principles will serve as reminders to help us sharpen our teaching skills to benefit THEM.

---

124   Holy Bible. New Living Translation. Tyndale: Carol Stream, 2004.

125   Holy Bible. Contemporary English Version. ABS: New York, 1995.

Communication tips for Bible teachers.

A. **Be studious.** This may seem very basic. But, you would be surprised at the number of ministers that try to "wing it," or the number of Sunday School teachers that try to "cram" on Saturday night. The Bible says in Acts 17:11, "These were more noble than those in Thessalonica, in that they received the word with all readiness of mind, and searched the scriptures daily, whether those things were so." So you must:

1. Study the available information related to your presentation. Know your material. Know the facts.

2. Never allow or suffer the embarrassment of inadequate preparation. You disqualify yourself and lose the respect of your audience as a result.

3. Organize your thoughts and align your body language and tone to support your words.

4. Choose your words carefully. Proverbs 15:23 says, "A man hath joy by the answer of his mouth: and a word spoken in due season, how good is it!"

5. Be careful of overly using meaningless words like "um" or "fillers" such as "Amen" and "praise God" or "thank you Jesus." To the onlooker, this can signify that you do not know what to say next or you have not studied.

B. **Be accurate.**

1. Whenever offering statistics, be sure that they are current and correct.

2. Do not exaggerate, allowing your enthusiasm to get the best of you.

C. **Be positive.**

1. Speak of those things which will inspire your listeners. Do not walk up before God's people as if the weight of the world is upon your shoulders. Be enthusiastic.

2. As a Bible teacher you shouldn't discuss church politics or controversies in your Bible lesson.[126] God's people are His "sheep," who need His Word. Those people who love controversy are often characterized as "goats." So, feed the sheep, not the goats.[127]

D. **Be sincere.**

1. If you get "stumped," do not pretend that you know the answer. Others already know that no one person knows it all. Tell the person that you will make every

---

126   Thuston, Bishop Lemuel F. Church Of God In Christ National Adjutancy. N.p., 1998.

127   Jakes, Bishop. T. D. N.d.

attempt to study and find the answer.

2. Speaking truthfully will increase your confidence. If you are not speaking from your heart, that will show in your body language. Body language is 90% of communication. Proverbs 23:7 says, "For as he thinketh in his heart, so is he: Eat and drink, saith he to thee; but his heart is not with thee."

E. **Be aware of your environment.** The "Four C's" will explain this point:

1. Context. The delivery method chosen must suit the circumstances and the needs of both the teacher and the listener.

2. Connect. The content of the message/teaching has to connect, on some level, with the already-held beliefs of the listener's.

    a. You may discover that your audience is misinterpreting or misunderstanding your words and ideas. Keep adjusting your communication until you are convinced that they are hearing what you are intending.

    b. To ensure that your message is heard, communicate by expressing your message from the point of view of the audience.

3.   Control. Try to control your defensiveness if you have a question and answer format. Fear of justifying behavior makes people hesitant to give feedback or receive from another person.

4.   Cues. When teaching, recognize that nonverbal cues can tell you:

    a.   When you have talked long enough.

    b.   When someone else wants to speak.

    c.   The mood of the crowd and their reaction to your remarks.

F.   Be professional in how you carry yourself. In this day and time presentation and "packaging" is everything. If you are timely, well groomed and carry yourself in a professional manner people are more apt to hear what you have to say.

How To Help People With God's Word

❀

LESSON 10:

HOW TO HELP YOUR LISTENERS

GROW IN THEIR FAITH

❀

LESSON 11:

HOW TO MINISTER TO MEN

"...And I, if and when I am lifted up from the earth,
will draw and attract all men to Myself."

- JOHN 12:27-32 -

(Amplified Bible AMP)

LESSON 10:

HOW TO HELP YOUR LISTENERS GROW IN THEIR FAITH

(Unless otherwise indicated all Scripture quotations are from the King James Version of the Holy Bible)

❋

CONTENTS:

INTRODUCTION

CHURCHES CAN GROW THROUGHT THE
PREACHING AND TEACHING OF GOD'S WORD

PRINCIPLES TO HELP YOUR LISTENERS GROW

I.
INTRODUCTION

(Unless otherwise indicated all Scripture quotations are
from the King James Version of the Holy Bible)

❋

WHAT IS THE PURPOSE OF THIS TEACHING?

The preaching and teaching of God's Word is important for the growth of the church, spiritually and numerically. But, before we go further, this writer does not want you to think that just because a church has a good Bible teaching program that it will automatically grow (there are many more factors too numerous to list in this book.

All of know of great Bible teachers who have very small followings. Or we know of great teachers of the Word who have followers that fail to grasp the message. Even Jesus had this difficulty with some of his followers in <u>Luke 24:25</u>, "Then he said unto them, O fools, and slow of heart to believe all that the prophets have spoken."

Nevertheless, one of the key factors to the growth of a church is a solid Biblical Studies program. This includes: Sunday School, Pastoral Teaching Night, etc. The instruction of God's Word must have a priority in the church.

Biblical Studies lead to a healthy church. And, church growth is the natural result of church health. Church health can only occur when our message is biblical and our mission balanced.[128]

The purpose of this teaching is to show pastors, preachers, Bible teachers and church leaders practical ways to make Biblical Studies effective; so that the church can grow spiritually and numerically.

CHURCHES ARE SUPPOSED TO GROW?

Every church is not going to be a "mega church." But, according to the Scriptures the church is to grow spiritually and numerically through Biblical Studies:

> **Acts 2:46-47.** And they, <u>continuing daily with one accord in the temple</u>, and breaking bread from house to house, did eat their meat with gladness and singleness of heart, Praising God, and having favour with all the people. And <u>the Lord added to the church</u> daily such as should be saved.

> **Acts 6:7.** And the <u>word of God increased</u>; and <u>the number of the disciples multiplied</u> in Jerusalem greatly; and a great company of the priests were obedient to the faith.

---

128   Warren, Rick. The Purpose Driven Church. Zondervan: Grand Rapids, 1995.

II.

CHURCHES CAN GROW THROUGH THE PREACHING AND TEACHING OF GOD'S WORD

❀

A BIBLE VERSE THAT WILL HELP
YOUR CHURCH TO GROW.

---

2 Peter 3:18. "But grow in grace, and in the knowledge of our Lord and Saviour Jesus Christ. To him be glory both now and forever. Amen."

---

2 PETER WILL HELP YOUR CHURCH TO GROW.

There are three reasons that the book of 2 Peter was written. All of it has to do with growing in grace:

A.   **To give you the confidence that it is God's will for you to grow in grace (2 Peter 1:10).** "Wherefore the rather, brethren, give diligence to make your calling and election sure: for if ye do these things, ye shall never fall."

B.   **To remind you of what it takes to grow in grace (2 Peter 1:12-13).** "12 Wherefore I will not be negligent to put you always in remembrance of these things, though ye know them, and be established in the present truth. **13** Yea, I think it meet, as long as I am in this tabernacle, to stir up you by putting you in remembrance."

C. **To stir up your mind to remember the Word; it is through the Word that you grow in grace (2 Peter 3:1).** "This second epistle, beloved, I now write unto you; in both which I stir up your pure minds by way of remembrance."

BIBLE STUDIES WILL CORRECT FALSE TEACHING

The author of 2 Peter was also trying to correct some false teaching that had slipped into the Church. In 2 Peter 2, he described the judgment that was going to come on these false teachers that taught that freedom in Christ meant that you could live a morally loose life. 2 Peter teaches that you can never grow grace while living an ungodly life. So, what exactly were the false teachers in 2 Peter instructing?

A. **They taught against believing in the Second Coming of Christ (2 Peter 3:3-4).** "3Knowing this first, that there shall come in the last days scoffers, walking after their own lusts, 4And saying, Where is the promise of his coming? For since the fathers fell asleep, all things continue as they were from the beginning of the creation."

B. **They misinterpreted Paul's teaching on freedom to mean that "anything goes" (2 Peter 3:16).** "As also in all his epistles, speaking in them of these things; in which are some things hard to be understood, which they that are unlearned and unstable wrest, as they do also the other scriptures, unto their own destruction."

2 PETER 3:18: GROW IN GRACE.

2 Peter 3:18 is really the summary of the book of 2 Peter: grow in grace. The entire book of 2 Peter is written to promote Christian growth and, again, to refute the false teaching that said that it was okay to live a morally loose life. As a matter of fact, the entire first chapter of 2 Peter is committed to the subject of how to grow in grace.[129]

A. The basis of Christian growth (2 Peter 1:1-4).

B. The way to Christian growth (2 Peter 1:5-9).

C. The consummation of Christian growth (2 Peter 1:10-15).

D. Christian growth and spiritual authority (2 Peter 1:16-21).

There are two interpretations of 2 Peter 3:18. Both of these interpretations are beneficial to our growth in Christ.

---

129   Unger, Merrill. The New Unger's Bible Handbook. Moody: Chicago, 1998.

A.   **Grow in grace.** This means that our growth is determined by God and our relationship with Him.

B.   **Grow in <u>the</u> grace.** This means that our growth is determined by our applying biblical instructions to our lives.

2 Peter teaches that we are to grow in grace and knowledgGrace and knowledge are the roots of Christian stability.[130]

A.   **What does it mean to grow (*auxano*)?**[131] To cause to increase. To become greater.[132] To increase in size and develop toward maturity.[133]

B.   **What does grace mean?** Grace is the generosity of God. It means that we have been called and elected to salvation by God's gift and power (see 2 Peter 1:10). It is through this massive gift that we are able to grow and mature.

C.   **The definition of knowledge.** Applying the truths of God's Word to your everyday life and thereby making yourself immune to error.[134]

---

130   Buttrick, George. The Interpreter's Bible Vol. XII. New York: Abingdon, 1953.

131   Strong, James. The Strongest Strong's. Zondervan: Grand Rapids, 2001.

132   Vine, W. E. Vine's Complete Expository Dictionary of Old and New Testament Words. Nelson: Nashville, 1996.

133   Mish, Frederick C. Webster's Ninth New Collegiate Dictionary. Webster: Springfield, 1989.

134   Buttrick, George. The Interpreter's Bible Vol. XII. New York: Abingdon, 1953.

III.
PRINCIPLES TO HELP YOUR LISTENERS GROW

❁

A.   **First, what am I growing towards?** The ultimate goal of growth in grace is to reach the standard of God's glory and excellence. While this may seem like an unreachable goal, God has given you everything necessary to reach this standard.

> **2 Peter 1:3.** According as his divine power hath given unto us all things that pertain unto life and godliness, through the knowledge of him that hath called us to glory and virtue...

B.   **There are three ways to grow in grace.**

1.   **The five-fold ministry was given to help you grow in grace (Ephesians 4:11-12).** "**11** And he gave some, apostles; and some, prophets; and some, evangelists; and some, pastors and teachers; **12** For the perfecting of the saints, for the work of the ministry, for the edifying of the body of Christ."

2.   **Knowledge of the Word of God (which comes through Biblical Studies) is the source of growing in grace.** Knowledge is described three ways in the book of 2 Peter.[135]

---

135   Buttrick, George. The Interpreter's Bible Vol. XII. New York: Abingdon, 1953.

a. **Knowledge of God (2 Peter 1:2).**

b. **Knowledge of Him that hath called us (2 Peter 1:3).**

c. **Knowledge of our Lord Jesus Christ (2 Peter 1:8).**

3. **You grow in grace by living consecrated.** The level of commitment to sin that you lived in, before knowing Christ, is the level of consecration to holiness that you should give God, once you become saved.[136]

Luke 12:48. "But he that knew not, and did commit things worthy of stripes, shall be beaten with few stripes. For unto whosoever much is given, of him shall be much required: and to whom men have committed much, of him they will ask the more."

C. **There are seven qualities that you need to develop, which will help you to grow in grace.**

1. **These seven qualities will ensure that you enter into the Kingdom of God.** According to the book of 2 Peter, Christ has passed down, through the apostles, truth that pertains to your salvation; however in order to grow you must develop what has been given to you (2 Peter 1:5-7).

---

136   Parker, Pastor Margaret. N.d.

By you developing the seven qualities found in 2 Peter 1:5-7, you are guaranteed an entrance into the kingdom of God.

2 Peter 1:10-11. "**10**Wherefore the rather, brethren, give diligence to make your calling and election sure: for if ye do these things, ye shall never fall: **11**For so an entrance shall be ministered unto you abundantly into the everlasting kingdom of our Lord and Saviour Jesus Christ."

2. **The seven qualities are found in 2 Peter 1:5-7.**[137] "5And beside this, giving all diligence, add to your faith virtue; and to virtue knowledge; 6And to knowledge temperance; and to temperance patience; and to patience godliness; 7And to godliness brotherly kindness; and to brotherly kindness charity."

1. **Virtue.** This means manliness, resolve or one who is armored and fortified for the struggle. The word can also mean excellence.

   a. **Knowledge.** Insight, intelligence or understanding of God's Word.

   b. **Temperance.** Power to endure difficulties. It also means self-control or the mastery of appetites, restraint in sensual impulses,

---

137   Buttrick, George. The Interpreter's Bible Vol. XII. New York: Abingdon, 1953.

especially sexual desires. Temperance is where desire becomes your servant and not your master.

c. **Patience.** The power to hold out in hope when life is difficult; a positive attitude of hope. This is a quality which causes you to refrain from giving in to suffering.

d. **Godliness.** Strong awareness and reverence of God's relation to every area of life; an attitude which4.75 in sees all things in their relation to God.

e. **Brotherly kindness.** The love that brothers of common descent have for one another. It is the avoidance of attitudes and practices that might destroy unity. Love for your neighbor and remembering the desperate needs of the community.

f. **Love.** General large heartedness which is characteristic of the Christian faith. This word is also used to describe God's consideration of the welfare of all people.

LESSON 11:

How To Minister To Men

(Unless otherwise indicated all Scripture quotations are from the King James Version of the Holy Bible)

❀

CONTENTS:

INTRODUCTION

WHAT DID JESUS SAY AND DO?

ADDRESSING THE CHALLENGE

DRAWING AND ATTRACTING MEN

I.
INTRODUCTION

(Unless otherwise indicated all Scripture quotations are from the King James Version of the Holy Bible).

❖

John 12:27-32 (Amplified Bible AMP)[138] *27 Now My soul is troubled and distressed, and what shall I say? Father, save Me from this hour [of trial and agony]? But it was for this very purpose that I have come to this hour [that I might undergo it].28 [Rather, I will say,] Father, glorify (honor and extol) Your [own] name! Then there came a voice out of heaven saying, I have already glorified it, and I will glorify it again.29 The crowd of bystanders heard the sound and said that it had thundered; others said, An angel has spoken to Him!30 Jesus answered, This voice has not come for My sake, but for your sake.31 Now the judgment (crisis) of this world is coming on [sentence is now being passed on this world]. Now the ruler (evil genius, prince) of this world shall be cast out (expelled).32 And I, if and when I am lifted up from the earth [on the cross], will draw and attract all men [Gentiles as well as Jews] to Myself.*

PURPOSE OF THIS LESSON.

As preachers and Bible teachers, we have to face the fact that, just by observation, many churches (of all races and denominations) are mostly made up of women and children. Also,

---

138   KJV*Amplified Holy Bible Parallel Bible. Zondervan: Grand Rapids, 1995.

the fact is the average man you run into, outside of the church, could care less about being inside of the church (no matter how much you preach hellfire and brimstone and the Second Coming). And, many of the men in the church are usually some type of title holder (pastor, elder, deacon, etc.); meaning you have even fewer men that are just regular everyday people.

Don't get this writer wrong; thank God for the "sisters." But, this is a problem, considering that Jesus was such an expert at drawing those of the masculine gender, along with women and children. It's a problem now to get men to volunteer in a local church; but Jesus had men who were willing to fight and die for His cause!

What happened? The fault cannot be in Jesus or the Gospel, it must be within us His Church. It may hurt us to say that; but sometimes we have to confront facts in order to bring about a change.

So the purpose of this message is for us to realize that there is a problem of a lack of men many churches. Start discussions about this subject [because there are very few sermons or Bible Studies that address this]. Briefly examine why many men say they don't want to have anything to do with church. Find some solutions from the Master at drawing men [Jesus]; so that we as preachers and Bible teachers may lead some lost soul [man, woman, boy or girl] to receive Christ Jesus as Lord and Savior.

II.

WHAT DID JESUS SAY AND DO?

❀

Now please realize this, when Jesus talked about "men," it is true that this term was, many times, generic for all people. So, for example, when He said, "...draw all men unto me," He was referring to drawing all people to Himself.

However, follow this train of thought for a minute: what you emphasize and speak about has some type of bearing on what you see in your life. The Word says in Proverbs 18:21 that, "Death and life are in the power of the tongue."

So even though Christ was out to win all souls (men, women, boys and girls), there had to be something that He said and did to attract men to Himself. The men He drew did not just "attend His church." But they left everything and were 100% devoted to Him to the end (in spite of their many failures). Look at this:

- Matthew 4:20. And they straightway left their nets, and followed him.

- Matthew 26:35. Peter said unto him, Though I should die with thee, yet will I not deny thee. Likewise also said all the disciples.

- Mark 10:28. Then Peter began to say unto him, Lo, we have left all, and have followed thee.

- **John 4:28-30, 39, 42.** [28] The woman then left her waterpot, and went her way into the city, and saith to the men, [29] Come, see a man, which told me all things that ever I did: is not this the Christ? [30] Then they went out of the city, and came unto him. [39] And many of the Samaritans of that city believed on him for the saying of the woman, which testified, He told me all that ever I did. [42] And said unto the woman, Now we believe, not because of thy saying: for we have heard him ourselves, and know that this is indeed the Christ, the Saviour of the world.

So going back to what Jesus "said," this writer believes that He reached men, because He talked about it; therefore that's what He saw manifested:

- Matthew 4:19. And he saith unto them, Follow me, and I will make you fishers of men.

- John 1:7. The same came for a witness, to bear witness of the Light, that all men through him might believe.

- John 5:23. That all men should honour the Son, even as they honour the Father. He that honoureth not the Son honoureth not the Father which hath sent him.

- John 12:32. And I, if I be lifted up from the earth, will draw all men unto me.

III.
ADDRESSING THE CHALLENGE

❀

CHURCH CONSIDERED A WOMAN'S CLUB?

Ask many men why they don't go to church, and they'll offer up words like **boring, irrelevant**, and **hypocrite.** Also, many men avoid anything that might call their manhood into question. This includes church, because many men believe that church is something for women and children, not men. Women comprise more than 60 percent of the typical adult congregation on any given Sunday.

However, a Man [Jesus] and His male disciples founded Christianity, most of Christianity's major saints and heroes were men. Men penned most of the New Testament books, and 95 percent of the senior pastors in the United States are men.

But, whenever large numbers of Christians gather, men are never in the majority. Not at revivals. Not at crusades. Not at conferences. Not at retreats. Not at concerts. With the exception of men's events and pastoral conferences, can you think of any large gathering of Christians that attracts more men than women?

Visit the church during the week, and you'll find most of the people working there are female. Drop in on a committee meeting, and you'll find a majority of the volunteers are women. Look over the leadership roster: the pastor is likely to be a man, but at least two-thirds of the ministry leaders will be women. Examine the sign-up sheets for volunteer work, prayer, Sunday school, and nursery duty. You'll be blessed if you see more than a couple of men's names on these lists.

Faithful women provide continuity in our congregations. Women are the devoted ones who build their lives around their commitments to Christ and His church. Women are more likely to teach and volunteer in church and are the greatest participants in Christian culture. With so much female presence and participation, the church has gained a reputation as a ladies' club in the minds of men.

WHERE ARE THE MANLY MEN?

Tough, earthy, working guys rarely come to church. High achievers, alpha males, risk takers, and visionaries are in short supply. Fun-lovers and adventurers are also underrepresented in church. Many times these rough-and-tumble men feel they don't fit in with the quiet, introspective gentlemen who populate the church today. The truth is most men in the pews grew up in church. Today's churchgoing man is humble, tidy, dutiful, and above all, nice.

What a contrast to the men of the Bible! Think of Moses and Elijah, David and Daniel, Peter and Paul. They were lions, not lambs— take-charge men who risked everything in service to God. They fought valiantly and spilled blood. They spoke their minds and stepped on toes. They were true leaders, tough guys who were feared and respected by the community. All of these men had two things in common:

they had an intense commitment to God, and they weren't what you'd call saintly. Such men seldom go to church today.

Furthermore, of the men who **do** attend church, most decline to invest themselves in the Christian life as their wives and mothers do. The majority of men attend services and nothing more.

Who is being touched by the Gospel today? Women. Women's ministries, women's conferences, women's Bible studies, and women's retreats are ubiquitous in the modern church. Men's ministry, if it even exists, might consist of an occasional pancake breakfast and an annual retreat.

THE CHALLENGE:
IF THE MEN ARE DEAD, THE CHURCH IS DEAD.[139]

How did a faith founded by a Man and His twelve male disciples become so popular with women, but such a turn-off to men? The early church was a magnet to males. Jesus' strong leadership, blunt honesty, and bold action mesmerized men. A five-minute sermon by Peter resulted in the conversions of three thousand men.

Today's church does not mesmerize men; it repels them. Just 35 percent of the men in the United States say they attend church weekly. Jesus built His church on twelve Spirit-filled men who changed the world. We must do the same. We **cannot have a thriving church without a core of men who are true followers of Christ. If the men are dead, the church is dead.**

---

139   Murrow, David. Why Men Hate Going To Church. Nelson: Nashville, 2005.

Some of the reasons men don't attend church

A. **Need for a more direct approach to life's issues.** Men tend to want to deal with "Reality" and "Tangible Solutions" the church is a place of faith & hope & on many occasions the churches answer to everyday problems is "pray" or P.U.S.H "Pray Until Something Happens" it's been the message since its inception and with men we tend to want and need something more direct something with more substance and the church is not providing this. Being faced with a problem and not having control or a direct solution or answer to end this problem does not sit well with men.

B. **Pimped Out Preachers.**[140] When you have church members who are struggling to pay rent, buy food, buy clothes and the church has been having a building fund for the past 35 years but yet the pastor of the church is driving the latest Cadillac, living in a mini mansion and has more gold than Fort Knox. Men tend look at him as a hustler (even though he may not be) and they don't want to be hustled themselves and some women tend to look at him as a man of God who has become successful in life because of his strong faith.

C. **Their fathers didn't attend church.** "Many men give their sons the impression that the church is not a place

---

140   Ibid.

for real men by stereotyping Christian men as passive, effeminate, and henpecked – qualities no man desires,"

D.   They have to work. When companies downsize and lay-offs lurk around every corner, men feel compelled to work as much as they can to provide some measure of security for their families. Neglecting their own spiritual growth is a small sacrifice for men who wish to keep their families out of dire straits.

E.   Too many collections. With rising unemployment, higher taxes, and other financial woes, the last thing any man wants to see when he goes to church is a pastor with his hand out asking for more than his fair share of his income.

F.   Services are too long and inflexible. Kenneth Davis says. "I know that going to church is important, but I like some time on Sundays to relax and do what I like to do."

G.   They have lost faith in God or do not believe in God. Men who grew up with a firm religious foundation have an easier time coping with adversity, but a test of faith sometimes can be enough to send even the most faithful servant fleeing from the fold.

H.   The church is hypocritical. Immoral behavior such as sexual misconduct and embezzlement by members, ministers and church leaders were cited as reasons why men avoid the church.

"I was appalled by all the backbiting and pettiness at my former church," says Eric Townshend, a 22 year-old student. "Those people were supposed to be Christians, but they sure didn't act like Christians. I feel that I exhibit the tenets of Christianity outside of church much better than many of those people who attend church religiously."

I.   **Insensitive pulpit.** Several of the men interviewed for this piece agreed that the church is unsympathetic to their plights. Since many men attend church to mend their battered egos, they get upset when the minister adds insult to injury by attacking them in his sermon. "By not attending church, men feel powerful and in control because they are finally able to challenge authority and get away with it," James says. "All any man wants to hear is that he is doing a good job. The church needs to be more sensitive to that fact.

IV.

DRAWING AND
ATTRACTING ALL MEN

❀

The last section was pretty blunt. But, as preachers and Bible teachers, we have to face the facts to change things. Thus far we have fulfilled the first three purposes of this lesson; now let's consider a few solutions. Here are some solutions that can be gleaned just from many of the Scriptures that are mentioned in this lesson.

A.   Don't have respect of persons, when it comes to drawing men and all souls (John 12:32 Amplified).[1] And I, if and when I am lifted up from the earth [on the cross], will draw and attract all men [Gentiles as well as Jews] to Myself.

B.   Allow God to make you a "fisher of men," because frankly, this is a challenge that only God can help us to solve (Matthew 4:19). And he saith unto them, Follow me, and I will make you fishers of men.

C.   Men, and everyone else, can smell a hypocrite. No matter how much preaching, teaching or discussing we do on this subject, people will avoid church when they see hypocrisy. The main witness is to LIVE THE LIFE (1 Peter 3:1-2 New

---

1   KJV*Amplified Holy Bible Parallel Bible. Zondervan: Grand Rapids, 1995.

Living Translation (NLT).[2] In the same way, you wives must accept the authority of your husbands. Then, <u>even if some refuse to obey the Good News, your godly lives will speak to them without any words. They will be won over [2] by observing your pure and reverent lives.</u>

D.   Don't just try to get men or lost souls committed to a certain pastor, church or denomination; get them committed to Jesus Christ and everything else will fall in place (Matthew 4:19). And he saith unto them, <u>Follow me</u>, and I will make you fishers of men.

---

2   Holy Bible. New Living Translation. Tyndale: Carol Stream, 2004.

How To Finish Strong

❋

LESSON 12:

HOW TO HAVE A FRUITFUL MINISTRY

"And thou shalt lay them up in the tabernacle of the con-
gregation before the testimony, where I will meet
with you. ⁵And it shall come to pass, that the man's
rod, whom I shall choose, shall blossom: ..."

- NUMBERS 17:4-8 -

❋

LESSON 13:

DONT GET DISTRACTED

"...Preach the word; be instant in season,
out of season; reprove, rebuke, exhort with
all long suffering and doctrine..."

- 2 TIMOTHY 4:1-5 -

LESSON 12:

How To Have A
Fruitful Ministry

*(Unless otherwise indicated all Scripture quotations are from
the King James Version of the Holy Bible)*

❋

CONTENTS:

INTRODUCTION

A SUMMARY OF THE BOOK OF NUMBERS

UNDERSTANDING NUMBERS

A GODLY AND FRUITFUL MINISTRY

I.
INTRODUCTION

(Unless otherwise indicated all Scripture quotations are from the King James Version of the Holy Bible).

❀

Numbers 17:4-8. 4*And thou shalt lay them up in the tabernacle of the congregation before the testimony, where I will meet with you.* 5*And it shall come to pass, that the man's rod, whom I shall choose, shall blossom: and I will make to cease from me the murmurings of the children of Israel, whereby they murmur against you.* 6*And Moses spake unto the children of Israel, and every one of their princes gave him a rod apiece, for each prince one, according to their fathers' houses, even twelve rods: and the rod of Aaron was among their rods.* 7*And Moses laid up the rods before the LORD in the tabernacle of witness.* 8*And it came to pass, that on the morrow Moses went into the tabernacle of witness; and, behold, the rod of Aaron for the house of Levi was budded, and brought forth buds, and bloomed blossoms, and yielded almonds.*

THE PURPOSE OF THIS LESSON

This teaching will show that while preachers and Bible teachers may face internal as well as external attacks from time to time; the key to remaining godly and fruitful is to maintain a fresh, daily and consistent walk with God. This is how Moses and Aaron were able to overcome some very serious challenges against their leadership, ministry and authority.

Important principles for ministering through challenges

A leader has two important characteristics: first, he is going somewhere; second, he is able to persuade other people to go with him. [3]

Followers in voluntary organizations cannot be forced to get on board. If the leader has no influence with them, then they won't follow. [4]

---

3   Zuck, Roy B. The Speaker's Quote Book. Kregel: Grand Rapids, 1997.

4   Maxwell, John C. Leadership 101. Nelson: Nashville, 2002.

II.

A SUMMARY OF
THE BOOK OF NUMBERS

❁

WHERE DOES THE NAME "NUMBERS" COME FROM?

Numbers covers thirty eight years in the history of Israel; the period of desert wandering in the Sinai Peninsula. It begins two years after the Exodus from Egypt. It ends on the eve of the entry into the Promised Land. The title comes from the *numbering* (or census) of Israel in Numbers 1 and 26.[5]

A NEW NATION MATURES

Israel as a nation is in its infancy at the beginning of this book. In Numbers (also known as the book of 'divine discipline'), it became necessary for the nation to go through the painful process of testing and maturation. God had to teach His people the consequences of irresponsible decisions. The forty years of wilderness experience transformed them from a group of ex-slaves into a nation ready to take the Promised Land.[6]

---

5   Alexander, David. Eerdman's Handbook to the Bible. Eerdman's: Grand Rapids, 1973.

6   Holy Bible. The Open Bible New King James Version. Nelson: Nashville,

Numbers is about "Mumblers"

Numbers tells of the murmuring and rebellion of God's people and of their subsequent judgment. Those whom God had redeemed from slavery in Egypt and with whom he had made a covenant at Mount Sinai responded not with faith, gratitude and obedience but with unbelief, ingratitude and repeated acts of rebellion, which came to extreme expression in their refusal to undertake the conquest of Canaan (see Numbers 14).[7]

2008.
7   Hoerber, Robert G. Concordia Self-Study Bible. Concordia: St. Louis, 1986.

III.
UNDERSTANDING NUMBERS 17

❁

A POWER STRUGGLE STARTED IN NUMBERS 16.

Korah, a prominent man, had a problem with Aaron's monopoly of the priesthood (Numbers 16:10b). Dathan and Abiram, also important men, challenged Moses on his failure to bring the Israelites into the Promised Land (Numbers 16:13-14). Really, their motive was to get Moses' position by virtue of their being descendents of Reuben, the oldest son of Jacob.[8]

God took this as a personal attack against Himself and therefore took responsibility for putting down this rebellion.[9] The Earth opened up and swallowed Dathan and Abiram together with their families. Korah also vanished with them. [Please note that Korah's family did not perish with him. And, some of his later descendants were godly people: Samuel and his grandson Heman].[10]

GOD'S CHOICE OF LEADERSHIP

In light of the rebellion in Numbers 16, God felt the need to give proof of His irrevocable choice of the Levites as ministers and

---

8   Schultz, Samuel J. The Old Testament Speaks. Harper: New York, 1980.

9   Alexander, David. Eerdman's Handbook to the Bible. Eerdman's: Grand Rapids, 1973.

10   Schultz, Samuel J. The Old Testament Speaks. Harper: New York, 1980.

the "Aaronites" as priests. He did not desire any further questioning of the authority of Israel's leaders.[11]

A rod or staff was usually the mark of a person of distinction, and each tribal leader would be likely to use a staff, perhaps even inscribed with his name.[12]

Among twelve rods (representing the tribes of Israel), that were presented before the Lord, He caused life to spring up in Aaron's rod alone. His rod budded (*parah*) which means to, "sprout, blossom or flourish."[13] This gave proof of God's choice for leaders.

Please note that Almond branches normally grow to maturity rapidly. Therefore, the growth of the almond blossoms on Aaron's staff also symbolized to the people that anyone who moved against Aaron's status as High priest would be punished swiftly.[14]

In addition to confirming Moses and Aaron and their divine appointments, the inscription of Aaron's name on this rod specifically designated him as the priest of Israel. Preservation of this rod in the Tabernacle served as permanent evidence of God's will.[15]

Did you know that Jesus is Aaron's Rod that Budded! The rod was a symbol of the ultimate leader: Jesus Christ. Because it pictures Christ's resurrection and He is also our great High Priest.[16]

---

11   Ibid.

12   Buttrick, Arthur George. The Interpreter's Bible Vol. II. New York: Abingdon, 1955.

13   Strong, James. Strong's Exhaustive Concordance of the Bible. Royal: Nashville, 1979.

14   Scherman, Rabbi Nosson. The Chumash. Mesorah: Brooklyn, 2003.

15   Schultz, Samuel J. The Old Testament Speaks. Harper: New York, 1980.

16   Unger, Merrill. The New Unger's Bible Handbook. Moody: Chicago, 1998.

IV.
A GODLY AND
FRUITFUL MINISTRY

❂

A GOD ORDAINED MINISTRY.

The display of God's choice for leadership occurred in front of the Testimony (or the Ark of the Covenant). Aaron's rod joined the stone tablets of the Law of Moses (Exodus 25:16) and the jar of manna (Exodus 16:33-34), within or near the Ark of the Covenant (Hebrews 9:4).

These holy symbols were ever present before the LORD as memorials to His special deeds in behalf of His people. Moreover, should anyone of a later age dare to question the unique and holy place of the Aaronic priests in the LORD's service, this symbolic memorial of God's choice of Aaron would stand in opposition to the culprits audacity.[17]

A PRAYING MINISTRY

It is miraculous that after this incident, Aaron's rod (placed within the Ark of the Covenant) remained in "blossom stage" for many years, even though it was later missing during Solomon's

---

[17]   Hoerber, Robert G. Concordia Self-Study Bible. Concordia: St. Louis, 1986.

day (I Kings 9:9).[18] Only prayer could have produced such an outstanding miracle.

WITH THIS IN MIND, WHAT DOES IT TAKE TO HAVE A GODLY AND FRUITFUL MINISTRY?

A. **A ministry can never be godly or fruitful if God has not ordained it.**

Korah, Dathan and Abiram were merely seeking the prestige and importance of ministry, just as many people do today. However, this ungodly motive led to their destruction. In contrast, the ministry of Moses and Aaron was fruitful for many years, because God had selected them to serve. John Maxwell has said, "True leadership cannot be awarded, appointed or assigned. It comes only from influence."[19]

B. **A ministry can only be as godly and fruitful as the prayer life of the minister.**

When this crisis first began against Moses' leadership, he did not try to retaliate or run a "smear campaign" against his enemies. Instead he "fell on his face" (Numbers 16:4). All through this problem Moses remained prayerful. This is why God later vindicated him.

---

18   Dake, Finnis Jennings. Dake's Annotated Reference Bible. Lawrenceville: Dake, 2001.

19   Maxwell, John C. Leadership 101. Nelson: Nashville, 2002.

The following illustration will show that your ministry cannot be any more successful, influential or powerful than your prayer life:

Two pastor's wives sat mending their husbands' pants. One of them said to the other, "My poor John, he is so discouraged in his church work. He said just the other day he was considering resigning. It seems nothing goes right for him."

The other replied, "Why, my husband was saying just the opposite. He is so enthused, it seems like the Lord is closer to him than ever before."

A hushed silence fell as they continued to mend the trousers; one patching the seat and the other the knees."[20]

PRAYER IS THE KEY TO HAVING A GODLY AND FRUITFUL MINISTRY

20   Hewett, James S. Illustrations Unlimited. Tyndale: Wheaton, 1988.

LESSON 13:

DON'T GET DISTRACTED

(Unless otherwise indicated all Scripture quotations are from the King James Version of the Holy Bible)

❀

CONTENTS:

NOTHING WORSE THAN
A DISTRACTED PREACHER

STAY FOCUSED

DON'T GET DISTRACTED

I.
NOTHING WORSE THAN
A DISTRACTED PREACHER!

*(Unless otherwise indicated all Scripture quotations are
from the King James Version of the Holy Bible)*

❖

2 Timothy 4:1-5. *4 I charge thee therefore before God,
and the Lord Jesus Christ, who shall judge the quick and the dead
at his appearing and his kingdom; 2 Preach the word; be instant
in season, out of season; reprove, rebuke, exhort with all long
suffering and doctrine. 3 For the time will come when they will not
endure sound doctrine; but after their own lusts shall they heap
to themselves teachers, having itching ears; 4 And they shall turn
away their ears from the truth, and shall be turned unto fables. 5
But watch thou in all things, endure afflictions, do the work of an
evangelist, make full proof of thy ministry.*

LESSON PURPOSE

In this dispensation the most important work that a
preacher or Bible teacher can involve themselves in, is the ministry
of soul winning. A soul is worth more value than the entire world
itself (Mark 8:36). Any saint, but especially the preacher and
Bible teacher should be a soul-winner. This lesson will, therefore,
encourage you not to get distracted from that mission.

A.   What does it mean to be distracted? To draw or direct

(as one's attention) to a different object or in different directions at the same time![21]

B. The Bible says a distracted person is unstable. <u>James 1:8</u>, "A double minded man is unstable in all his ways."

C. A distracted person can even be deadly! Distracted driving is a dangerous epidemic on America's roadways. In 2010 alone, over 3,000 people were killed in distracted driving crashes.[22] What's even worse is when you have a preacher or Bible teacher that is distracted from their mission. This is why Paul said to stay focused by doing "the work of an evangelist, make full proof of thy ministry."

---

21   Mish, Frederick C. Webster's Ninth New Collegiate Dictionary. Webster: Springfield, 1989.

22   http://www.distraction.gov/. (Accessed, June 14, 2012).

II.
STAY FOCUSED
❁

It is a terrible thing when a minister is distracted from preaching the Gospel and winning souls! This is why Paul told Timothy to stay focused and not get distracted.

A.   Paul was Timothy's mentor. If you are going to stay focused as a preacher or Bible teacher; it is important that you associate with seasoned ministers who are focused on the prize. Paul had three associations: Gamaliel was his teacher, Barnabas was his brother in the Lord, and Timothy was his son in the Gospel. Every preacher needs these associations:

1.   Gamaliel. Someone to mentor you.

2.   Barnabas. A brother in the Lord.

3.   Timothy. Someone for you to mentor. (Note: of course here you have to live a life that is worth following).

B.   The book of 2 Timothy.[23] This letter was written a year after 1 Timothy. Paul was in Rome and for a second time he was a prisoner. Here Paul asked Timothy to come to him before winter, and to bring Mark with him.

C.   2 Timothy 4:1-5. Paul was anticipating that he would die soon, so he encouraged his "son Timothy" to a faithful dis-

---

23   http://www.biblegateway.com/resources/eastons-bible-dictionary/Timothy-Second-Epistle. (Accessed, May 28, 2012).

charge of all the duties of his ministry. He told Timothy to be serious about his duties, stay focused and don't get distracted because he also would one day appear before the Judge of the living and the dead.

D. You must also stay focused because your job is SO important!

1. You are the laborer (Matthew 9:38)! Take note that very rarely if at all will you find Jesus telling us to pray for God to save. Instead He told us that the harvest was plenteous; but the laborers were few. Therefore, he said to pray for laborers to go out into the harvest and work!

2. How can they hear without you (<u>Romans 10:14</u>)? How then shall they call on him in whom they have not believed? And how shall they believe in him of whom they have not heard? And how shall they hear without a preacher?

III.
DON'T GET DISTRACTED

❁

A.   Don't get distracted; because it may cost you your own soul (Luke 9:62)! And Jesus said unto him, No man, having put his hand to the plough, and looking back, is fit for the kingdom of God.

B.   Don't get distracted; because JESUS (your perfect example) never got distracted!

1.   Luke 9:51-53. And it came to pass, when the time was come that he should be received up, he stedfastly set his face to go to Jerusalem, ⁵² And sent messengers before his face: and they went, and entered into a village of the Samaritans, to make ready for him. ⁵³ And they did not receive him, because his face was as though he would go to Jerusalem.

2.   Luke 13:22. And he went through the cities and villages, teaching, and journeying toward Jerusalem.

3.   He stayed focused until He made it to the Cross!

ABOUT THE AUTHOR

❂

Dr. Elijah H. Hankerson III holds a Bachelor of Arts (Evangel University, of the Assemblies of God), a Master of Arts (Assemblies of God Theological Seminary) and a Doctorate of Divinity (Academy of Theology). He also founded the Institute of Ministerial Excellence and Training. He has been mentored under five great leaders: the late Dr. Elijah H. Hankerson I, the late Bishop T. L. Westbrook, the late Bishop E. Harris Moore, Bishop R. J. Ward, and Presiding Bishop Charles E. Blake, Sr.

He has 22 years of pastoral experience and has been in the ministry for 27 years. He is the Senior Pastor and founder of the Life Center International C.O.G.I.C. of Saint Louis, MO, which has 500 members. Prior to this he pastored the Christ Temple C.O.G.I.C. and later the Timmons Temple C.O.G.I.C., both of Springfield, MO. While serving Timmons Temple, Dr. Hankerson served on the Sherman Avenue Area Project Committee, the Spiritual Life Committee of Evangel University, and also founded the Ann Hankerson Community Development Center.

Dr. Hankerson is active in the Missouri Eastern First Jurisdiction (Church Of God In Christ) as an Administrative Assistant and founding Superintendent of the Robert C. Williams District; overseeing 25 churches, with missions work to 50 churches on the continent of Africa. He also serves on the board of directors, ordination board and grievance committee. His past years of service to the jurisdiction formerly include serving as: Special Assistant to the Bishop, Vice Chairman of District Superintendents, program committee member and former Chairman of the Public Relations Department. He has preached in many Holy Convocations throughout the United States; including having the honor of preaching "Official Day" for Bishop R. J. Ward on two occasions.

Internationally he has served in the Church Of God In Christ as: President of the Department of Evangelism, Representative of the General Board to the General Assembly; Coordinator of both the 40 day consecration preceding the International Holy Convocation, and also the 50 day Pilgrimage to Pentecost; Board Member of Jubilee Broadcasting Network; Vice Chairman of Vision Week. His past commitments to the church have been: founding Executive Board member and former Director of Public Relations for COGIC Urban Initiatives, Inc.; member of the Holy Convocation program committee; member of the Tri-Jurisdictional Liaison Committee; Point Person for the Soul Winning Ministry; member of the Constitution Committee of the General Assembly; Deputy to the Commissioner of Technology and Media and member of the Committee to host the Holy Convocation in St Louis, MO. He has also authored literature and served on the election campaign of a host of national officers. Dr. Hankerson has also had the distinct honor of preaching for Presiding Bishop Charles E. Blake, Sr., on many occasions, at the world renowned West Angeles Church of God in Christ in Los Angeles, CA; and he also preached as a keynote speaker in both the 104th International Holy Convocation and the 106th International Holy Convocation.

Heavily involved in the community, Dr. Hankerson has the distinct honor of serving as the elected 1st Vice President of the Saint Louis Metropolitan Clergy Coalition. He is a "Life Member" of the NAACP, member of the distinguished Charmaine Chapman Society and is an active member of both the Northside Neighborhood Action Association and the Police Department's Sixth District Community Outreach. He has served in times past as a coordinator of the monthly clergy meeting with the mayor of Saint Louis, reelection campaign committee for Mayor Francis Slay; participant of the monthly meeting with the superintendent of St. Louis Public Schools. He has also had the privilege of giving the keynote address for the citywide Dr. Martin Luther King, Jr. holiday celebrations, for both the cities of Springfield, Missouri and Saint Louis, Missouri; he has been named an "Honorary Chair" of the annual Saint Louis celebration. He has received numerous awards and honors: including a resolution from the Missouri State Senate, offered by (former state senator) Congressman William Lacy Clay, Jr. and two resolutions from the Board of Alderman of the city of Saint Louis. He has also had the privilege of serving in the motorcade for President Barack Obama.

Throughout his years of ministry Dr. Hankerson has had the honor of serving with various ecumenical bodies including: staff member, Joyce Meyer Ministries; "12 priests," Juanita Bynum Ministries/Midwest Regional Prayer Revival; Co-Chair, Gateway Call/Donnie McClurkin Ministries, board member Anointed Music Ministries and executive board member, Gateway Kingdom Ministries.

Believing in the impact of media ministry, Dr. Hankerson initiated the Life Center Radio Program and the Keys for Life Television Program. He also previously wrote a monthly column in Sparkman Magazine, entitled "Ask the Doctor," and has been a guest on both the Trinity Broadcasting Network and the Word Network.

Dr. Hankerson has travelled extensively, including: 49 states, and has been blessed to see 9 countries. He has preached the Gospel in Jerusalem, Israel; and was later sent to Israel again by the American Israel Education Foundation for study and research.

The love and inspiration of Dr. Hankerson's life is his lovely wife, Evangelist Rachel L. Hankerson and their three children: Elijah IV, Raquel and Matthew, who are 5th generation members of the Church Of God In Christ.

BIBLIOGRAPHY

❀

Alexander, David. Eerdman's Handbook to the Bible. Eerdman's: Grand Rapids, 1973.

Bell, James Stuart and Stan Campbell. The Complete Idiot's Guide to the Bible. Penguin: New York, 2005.

Bruce, F. F. The Epistle to the Hebrews. Eerdmans: Grand Rapids, 1990.

Buttrick, Arthur George. The Interpreter's Bible Vol. II. New York: Abingdon, 1955.

Buttrick, George. The Interpreter's Bible Vol. XII. New York: Abingdon, 1953.

Buttrick, Arthur George. The Interpreter's Dictionary of The Bible. New York: Abingdon, 1962.

Carson, Ben, Think Big. Zondervan: Grand Rapids, 1992.

Carter, Tom. From the Writings of Charles H. Spurgeon. Baker: Grand Rapids, 1988.

Clarke, W. K. Concise Bible Commentary. MacMillan: New York, 1953.

Cutshall, Bryan. "Twin Rivers Worship Center." Twin Rivers: Saint Louis, 2009.

Collins, Louanne (1996). Macclesfield Sunday School 1796-1996. Macclesfield, Cheshire: Macclesfield Museums Trust.

Dake, Finnis Jennings. Dake's Annotated Reference Bible. Lawrenceville: Dake, 2001.

"Defining Evangelicalism." Institute for the Study of American Evangelicals, Wheaton College. http://isae.wheaton.edu/defining-evangelicalism/. Retrieved August 31, 2011.

D. J. D. Davis Dictionary of the Bible. Royal: Nashville, 1973.

Dollar, Creflo A. 8 Steps To Create The Life You Want. Faith Words: New York, 2008.

Easton, M. G. Illustrated Bible Dictionary, Third Edition. Nelson: Grand Rapids, 1897.

Foster, Richard. Celebration of Discipline. Harper: Cambridge: 1978.

Hagee, John. The Seven Secrets. Charisma: Lake Mary, 2004.

Hagin, Jr., Kenneth. I Cannot Be Defeated and I Will Not Quit. Rhema: Tulsa, 2001.

Hagin, Kenneth E. Praying To Get Results. Rhema: Tulsa, 1983.

Henry, Matthew. Matthew Henry's Commentary
on the Whole Bible: Complete and Unabridged in
One Volume. Hendrickson: Peabody, 2008.

Hewett, James S. Illustrations Unlimited. Tyndale: Wheaton, 1988.

Hill, Brennan; Paul F. Knitter, William Madges.
Faith, Religion & Theology: A Contemporary
Introduction. Twenty-Third Publications.

Hoerber, Robert G. Concordia Self-Study
Bible. Concordia: St. Louis, 1986.

Holloway, James. God's Way to Become a Warrior.
Solomon's Temple: St Louis, 2003.

Holy Bible. Amplified Version. Zondervan: Grand Rapids, 1987.

Holy Bible. Contemporary English Version. ABS: New York, 1995.

Holy Bible. New Living Translation. Tyndale: Carol Stream, 2004.

Holy Bible. The Open Bible New King James
Version. Nelson: Nashville, 2008.

Horn, Ken. "The Azusa Street Revival." Pentecostal
Evangel. General Council: Springfield, May 31, 1998.

Jakes, Bishop. T. D. N.d.

KJV*Amplified Holy Bible Parallel Bible.
Zondervan: Grand Rapids, 1995.

http://www.biblegateway.com/resources/eastons-bible-dictionary/Timothy-Second-Epistle. (Accessed, May 28, 2012).

http://blackandmarriedwithkids.com/2010/09/7-reasons-why-men-dont-attend-church/. (Accessed, July 13, 2012).

http://blackmenchronicles.blogspot.com/2011/06/why-dont-black-men-dont-go-to-church.html. (Accessed, July 13, 2012).

http://christianity.about.com/od/easternorthodoxy/p/orthodoxpro-file.htm. (Accessed, September 29, 2012).

http://www.distraction.gov/. (Accessed, June 14, 2012).

http://en.wikipedia.org/wiki/Book_of_romans. (Accessed, February 11, 2011).

http://en.wikipedia.org/wiki/Footwashing. (Accessed, September 9, 2009).

http://www.foursquare.org/about/our_purpose. (Accessed, February 11, 2011).

http://www.fullgospelbaptist.org/. (Accessed, February 11, 2011).

http://www.webcitation.org/query?url=http://www.geocities.com/ Athens/Parthenon/6528/fundcont.htm&date=2009-10-25+06:18:43. (Accessed, September 29, 2012).

http://www.zenit.org/rssenglish-29058. Retrieved 2 May 2010.

Maxwell, John C. Leadership 101. Nelson: Nashville, 2002.

Maxwell, John. The Maxwell Leadership Bible. Nelson: Nashville, 2007.

Maxwell, John C. The Power of Influence. RiverOak: Tulsa, 2001.

McBriean, Richard P. The HarperCollins Encyclopedia of Catholicism. HarperCollins.

McGhee, Gary. "The Holy Spirit Falls at Topeka." Pentecostal Evangel. General Council: Springfield, May 31, 1998.

Mish, Frederick C. Webster's Ninth New Collegiate Dictionary. Webster: Springfield, 1989.

Murren, Doug. The Baby Boomerang. Regal: Ventura, 1990.

Murrow, David. Why Men Hate Going To Church. Nelson: Nashville, 2005.

"Number of Catholics on the Rise". Zenit News Agency. 27 April 2010.

Parker, Pastor Margaret. N. d.

Peterson, Eugene E. The Message. NAV: Colorado Springs, 2005.

Range, C. F. Official Manual of the Doctrines and Discipline of the Church Of God In Christ. COGIC Publishing House: Memphis, 1973.

Scherman, Rabbi Nosson. The Chumash. Mesorah: Brooklyn, 2003.

Schultz, Samuel J. The Old Testament Speaks. Harper: New York, 1980.

"Spirit and Power: A 10-Country Survey of Pentecostals", Executive Summary. The Pew Forum on Religion and Public Life.

Strong, James. The Strongest Strong's. Zondervan: Grand Rapids, 2001.

"The Anglican Communion Official website - Provincial Registry". Anglicancommunion.org. http://www.anglicancommunion.org/tour/index.cfm. Retrieved 2012-07-20.

The English Reformation by Professor Andrew Pettegree. Bbc.co.uk.

Thompson, Frank Charles. Thompson Chain Reference Bible. Thompson: Post Falls, n.d.

Thompson, Robb. Excellence in the Workplace. Family Harvest: Tinley Park, 2002.

Thuston, Bishop Lemuel F. Church Of God In Christ National Adjutancy. N.p., 1998.

Trimm, Dr. Cindy N. Binding the Strong Man. Kingdom Life: Ft Lauderdale, 2005.

Unger, Merrill. The New Unger's Bible Handbook. Moody: Chicago, 1998.

Van Crouch Communications. The C.E.O.'s Little Instruction Book. Trade Life: Tulsa, 1999.

Vaughn, Willie L. Study Guide and Review for Ordination of Licensed Ministers and Evangelist Missionary Licensing: Church Of God In Christ. Western Missouri Jurisdiction: 1997.

Vine, W. E. Vine's Complete Expository Dictionary of Old and New Testament Words. Nelson: Nashville, 1996.

Warren, Rick. The Purpose Driven Church. Zondervan: Grand Rapids, 1995.

White, L. Michael. From Jesus To Christianity. Harper: NY, 2004.

Zodhiates, Spiros. The Complete Word Study New Testament. AMG: Chattanooga, 1991.

Zuck, Roy B. The Speaker's Quote Book. Kregel: Grand Rapids, 1997.

www.ingramcontent.com/pod-product-compliance
Lightning Source LLC
La Vergne TN
LVHW051514080426
835509LV00017B/2055